About the Author

Born in Germany, Edgar Rothermich studied music and sound engineering at the prestigious Tonmeister program at the University of Arts in Berlin where he graduated in 1989 with a Master's Degree. He worked as a composer and music producer in Berlin and moved to Los Angeles in 1991 where he continued his work on numerous projects in the music and film industry ("The Celestine Prophecy", "Outer Limits", "Babylon 5", "What the Bleep do we know", "Fuel", "Big Money Rustlas").

For the past 20 years Edgar has had a successful musical partnership with electronic music pioneer and founding Tangerine Dream member Christopher Franke. Recently in addition to his collaboration with Christopher, Edgar has been working with other artists as well as on his own projects.

In 2010 he started to release his solo records in the "Why Not ..." series with different styles and genres. The current releases are "Why Not Solo Piano", "Why Not Electronica", "Why Not Electronica Again", and "Why Not 90s Electronica". This previously unreleased album was produced in 1991/1992 by Christopher Franke. All albums are available on Amazon and iTunes including the 2012 release, the re-recording of the Blade Runner Soundtrack.

In addition to composing music, Edgar Rothermich is writing technical manuals with a unique style, focusing on rich graphics and diagrams to explain concepts and functionality of software applications under his popular GEM series (Graphically Enhanced Manuals). His bestselling titles are available as printed books on Amazon, as Multi-Touch eBooks on the iBookstore and as pdf downloads from his website. (languages: English, Deutsch, Español, 简体中文)

www.DingDingMusic.com   GEM@DingDingMusic.com

About the GEM (Graphically Enhanced Manuals)

UNDERSTAND, not just LEARN

What are Graphically Enhanced Manuals? They're a new type of manual with a visual approach that helps you UNDERSTAND a program, not just LEARN it. No need to read through 500 of pages of dry text explanations. Rich graphics and diagrams help you to get that "aha" effect and make it easy to comprehend difficult concepts. The Graphically Enhanced Manuals help you master a program much faster with a much deeper understanding of concepts, features and workflows in a very intuitive way that is easy to understand.

About the Formatting

Green colored text indicates Key Commands. I use the following abbreviations: **sh** (shift key), **ctr** (control key), **opt** (option key), **cmd** (command key). A plus (+) between the keys means that you have to press all those keys at the same time. *sh+opt+K* means: Press the K key while holding down the shift and option key.

Brown colored text indicates Menu Commands with an arrow (➤) indicating submenus.
Edit ➤ Source Media ➤ All means Click on the Edit Menu, scroll down to Source Media and select "All" from the submenu.

Blue arrows indicate what happens if you click on an item or popup menu ●━━━➤

About the Editor

Many thanks to Chas Ferry for editing and proofreading my manuals. www.hollywoodtrax.com

The manual is based on Final Cut Pro X v10.0.9
Manual: Print Version 2013-0808

ISBN-13: 978-1463775261
ISBN-10: 1463775261
Copyright © 2013 Edgar Rothermich

Table of Contents

"Final Cut Pro X" is a major upgrade of Apple's successful video editing software "Final Cut Pro".

When it was released in the Summer of 2011, it created quite the sensation. Unfortunately, it wasn't for its ground breaking new approach. Many professional editing features were missing in the original 1.0 version and some of the new concepts didn't resonate very well with the user base. Although Apple kept its promise that more features would come in future releases, there is still some anger in the Final Cut community and many users switched to different software or tried to stay with the now discontinued FCP7 version as long as possible.

This is very unfortunate. All that bad press and those heated discussions about "the end" of Apple's professional video editing software overlooked one very important detail:

Final Cut Pro X is an amazing NEW piece of software.

This manual will help you learn and more importantly, fully understand the new concepts behind Final Cut Pro X.

As I explained in the preface, my approach in writing manuals is to provide a visual understanding to create a better foundation for the actual learning process of the application. This is even more important with an innovative product like Final Cut Pro X.

It is often harder to learn a similar software (or hardware) than a brand new one because it first requires some sort of "un-learning" of existing concepts and workflows that one has become accustomed to. Those misconceptions caused some of the frustrations among the FCP7 users. Please note, FCPx is not similar to FCP7, it is a brand new program! It is understandable that Apple wanted to keep the established brand name of "Final Cut Pro" with their new release, but they didn't emphasize enough that FCPx is not just an upgrade.

Releasing a FCPx manual that just tells you where to click now in order to do the same process as in FCP7 wouldn't do it any justice. Trying to use an existing workflow can be frustrating when it doesn't work with a new application. This is often not the fault of the application itself. I hope my diagrams will help to understand "why" you have to click somewhere and not just "where". Yes, it requires a little time investment from the user, but my visual approach will make it easy to reach that level of understanding.

Once you're there, everything else will fall into place and you will master Final Cut Pro X, realizing that this is truly a professional piece of editing software.

Once you use the new concepts and features, you might not only like them but may find that they could speed up your workflow tremendously.

This is the second edition of my popular FCPx book that includes all the new features that were introduced in the major FCPx updates of 10.0.3 and 10.0.6. This made the third book that I had released (**Final Cut Pro X - 10.0.3 New Features**") obsolete because all those features are now included in the new editions.

I still spread the FCPx content across two books:

- **"Final Cut Pro X - How it Works"** covers all the basics. It introduces the new concepts and interface elements along with the main editing features.

- **"Final Cut Pro X - The Details"** covers all the rest of the features in greater detail. More importantly, the manual provides a much deeper understanding of the program and explains the underlying architecture of its databases and metadata. This is the new foundation that sets FCPx apart from the rest of the video editing software.

As you might have noticed, I use the abbreviation "FCPx" and "FCP7" throughout the manuals.

Get the app

Along with the new FCPx version came a new distribution model for the application.

Apple doesn't sell its software on physical discs anymore. All their apps are now available only through downloads from the various online Apple Stores or from their website.

Free Trial Version

Before you purchase FCPx, you can go to Apple's website and download a 30-day Free Trial version of the full featured FCPx app.

Purchase from the Mac App Store

To purchase the app, you go through the same steps as with any other app purchases from the App Store

☑ Go to the Mac App Store on your computer *Apple Menu ➤ App Store...*

☑ Sign in with your Apple ID.

☑ Click the $299.99 price tag and follow the steps.

☑ The app will be downloaded to your computer.

One big advantage of the App Store system is that your purchase is registered with the Apple ID account that you made the purchase with. That means you can download the app to any computer that is signed in with the same Apple ID you made the purchase with. Any available update will also be available from the App Store application which makes it easy to stay current with the latest version of any app.

Additional Downloads

However, there is a disadvantage to the new online distribution model. You don't get a printed manual anymore and additional files in the 10s of gigabytes have to be downloaded over the internet.

➡ *Documentation*

The official Documentation for FCPx is available through the built-in Help Center (from the FCPx Help Menu) and on the FCPx website. Both require an internet connection.
The downloadable pdf file is available at http://manuals.info.apple.com/en_US/final_cut_pro_x_user_guide.pdf

Help Center
Help ➤ Final Cut Pro X Help

FCPx website
http://help.apple.com/finalcutpro/mac/10.0.6/

➡ *Additional Content*

The size of the initial download for FCPx is already 1.6GB. Any additional files like effects or video codecs can be downloaded afterwards once you launched the app. The Final Cut Pro menu provides a command "*Download Additional Content...*" that opens the App Store application and displays any files that are available for download.

Requirements

As with any CPU intensive app, the better your machine, the better your overall experience. Here are the bare minimum requirements to run FCPx.

- ▶ Mac computer with an Intel Core 2 Duo processor or better.
- ▶ 2GB of RAM (4GB of RAM recommended).
- ▶ OpenCL-capable graphics card or Intel HD Graphics 3000 or later.
- ▶ 256MB of VRAM (512MB of VRAM recommended).
- ▶ Display with 1280-by-768 resolution or higher.
- ▶ OS X v10.6.8 or OS X v10.7.5 or OS X v10.8.2 or later.
- ▶ 2.4GB of disk space.

As with any other Mac application, the localized versions are incorporated in the app and don't require any additional download. FCPx follows whatever language you are logged in in OSX and displays the app in that language. The supported language as of version 10.0.8 are:

- 💡 English, German, French, Japanese, Chinese

After downloading FCPx and launching it the first time, it will look something like this.

Final Cut Pro X

The user interface might not look familiar if you are used to earlier FCP versions. As I mentioned already, FCPx introduces some new concepts and workflows, so I want to go over some basics first.

Digital Video Editor - Workflow

The main workflow in FCPx is basically the same as with any other Digital Video Editors even FCP7. We can break it down into 5 steps:

❶ **Import** the Media Files into FCPx. Whatever source material you want to use (video, audio, images) has to be imported into the application first. The files are now collected in an area called the "**Event**".

❷ **Organize** the Media Files (as Event Clips) in a specific way to make it easy and fast to preview and select the right Clips. This is done in FCPx now in the **Event** window.

❸ **Place** the chosen Clips onto a Timeline in a sequence which will become the movie. This area is now called "**Project**".

❹ **Edit** the Clips on the Timeline to fine tune the sequence by using effects and other creative tools. Expect major changes here too.

❺ **Export (Share)** the Timeline as the final movie.

Video Editing: FCPx Workflow

Organize your Clips in the
Event Browser

Edit the Clips on the
Timeline

Getting Media Files into
FCPx

Event

Select which Clips to
place on the Timeline

Project

Export the final movie

❶   ❷   ❸   ❹   ❺

Where are the Documents?

The first and one of the biggest changes in FCPx is with the application itself, or more accurately "the kind of application" it is. Because this change has a big impact (some would say limitation) when using FCPx, I want to go into the details a bit first.

Although all application files look the same on the "outside" (there is an icon in the Applications folder that you double click and the application launches), there are two types of apps, "**Document-based**" and "**non Document-based**". Most Document-based apps let you create "something", i.e. Word, Excel, Photoshop, FCP7, etc. What they have in common is that the app is a tool that enables you to create and edit some sort of a document that is separate from the app. That could be a word document, a spreadsheet, a song or even a movie. In a non Document-based app there is no document to open or save. Everything is contained within the app. iTunes, iPhoto or Calendar don't have documents that you can open or save. All the data exists as part of the app and everything is there when you launch the app.

Here is a diagram that shows the document in relationship to its application that it created:

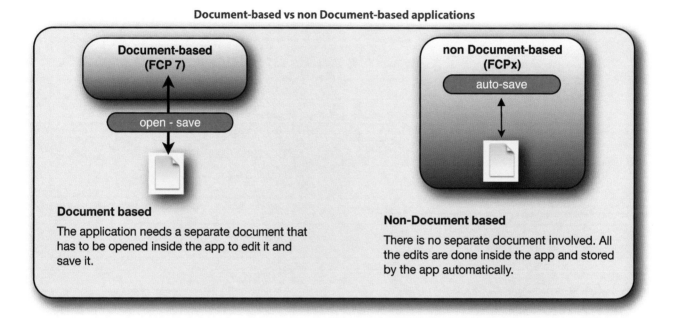

The reason I bring up the concept of Document-based vs non Document-based is to understand **why** FCPx works in the way it does. Having no Project Files and no Open or Save command is not just a decision about specific features. It is based on the fundamental change of the underlying concept in FCPx compared to FCP7 or other video editing software.

➡ **Auto Save**

Any changes or edits you'll do in FCPx will automatically be saved to the "invisible" Project File. However, this is not a typical "Auto Save" feature. Other Document-based apps provide an auto save feature which automatically presses the Save button for you to save a document, mostly based on a time interval.

However, the auto-save functionality in FCPx is more like the "auto-save" feature in iTunes or iPhoto. For example, every time you make changes in iTunes (create a Playlist or add keywords to a Song), those changes are saved. However, you don't think of it as a typical auto-save. It just happens and it will be saved. Any time you quit iTunes and open it the next time, whatever changes you made, will be there. That is how you can think of the new auto-save functionality in FCPx.

Here is a comparison chart for a Document-based app (FCP7) vs a non Document-based app (FCPx)

Document-based	non Document-based
Launching the application just launches the "app" without the document.	Launching the application itself is all that's required. All the "stuff" will be there.
You have to open a document, edit it and save it.	The app doesn't have an Open or Save command. Again, everything will be there at launch.
All the changes have to be saved to a document.	All the changes are automatically saved to a specific file that the application handles without the user's interaction.
Documents can be stored anywhere in the file system. Just open the Open Dialog window and navigate to any location on your drive.	The files that are required by the app and handled by the app usually have to be in a specific directory. The user doesn't have to know it because he is not expected to alter them directly.
It is easy and transparent to move documents around between computers. The only requirement is that the computer has the app installed that is needed to open the document.	Moving "documents" around can be tricky because they are "hidden" by the app. Special (new) file management procedures have to be learned and applied.
Examples: **FCP 7**, Word, Excel, Pages	Examples: **FCPx**, iTunes, iWeb, Calendar

File Management: FCP7 vs FCPx

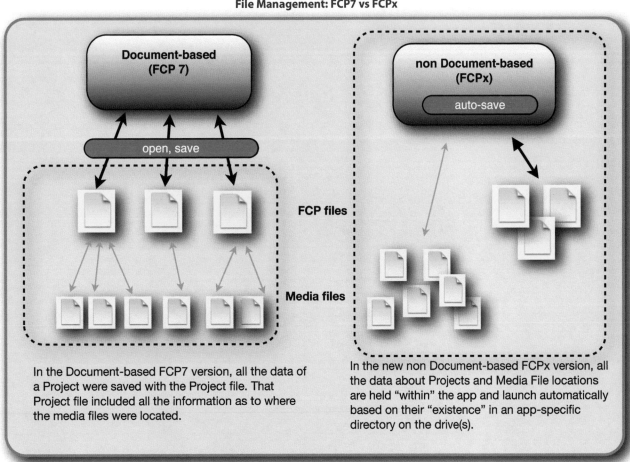

In the Document-based FCP7 version, all the data of a Project were saved with the Project file. That Project file included all the information as to where the media files were located.

In the new non Document-based FCPx version, all the data about Projects and Media File locations are held "within" the app and launch automatically based on their "existence" in an app-specific directory on the drive(s).

Basic Concept

After understanding that FCPx is now a non Document-based application (almost like a database), we can go to the next step and look at the basic concept of the application.

Think of FCPx as an eco-system with two main components:

❶ The FCPx app itself represented by the Graphical User Interface (GUI)

❷ The app specific location of the FCPx files on the hard drive(s)

With the new "strictly enforced policies", FCPx lets you concentrate on the first element, the GUI. Everything can be managed from here without an extra trip to the Finder to manage the files outside the GUI. You can stay "inside" the GUI all the time ❶. All the Media Files on your hard drive that you have imported into FCPx are linked to an Event inside FCPx and all the work you do inside FCPx is saved automatically to the hard drive to specific folders ❷. Even more complex file management tasks can be performed later inside the FCPx GUI.

The Import procedure is the "entrance" into that eco-system. The Export procedure is where you "leave" the system when your project is done and you save a final video to a new QuickTime video file or "share" it to another destination.

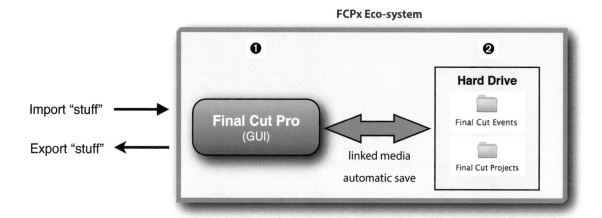

Basic Elements: Events - Projects

The previous diagram displays the two folders that FCPx creates and uses to store all its data. The FCPx application is "connected" to those two folders. All of the data that FCPx manages (invisible to the user) are stored in those two folders (more details bout that later):

- 💡 **Final Cut Events**
- 💡 **Final Cut Project**

Those two folders also represent the two main elements in FCPx and dominant in the FCPx user interface:

Here is the diagram with the basic workflow again showing those two elements:

The Event area and the Project area are the two main elements in FCPx. They build the foundation of the FCPx workflow, therefore it is crucial to fully understand their specific functionality. First, here are some basic rules and workflows that I will explain step by step throughout the manual.

➡ *Event*

- Media Files have to be imported as Clips into an Event. Every Clip in FCPx has to belong to an Event.
- In the Event area, you organize the Clips, rename them and add additional information (reel, scenes, etc).
- In the Event area, you add Metadata to the Clips (ratings, keywords, ...) to create Subclips and searchable keywords.
- The Event area is the source for Clips to be used in the Project.

➡ *Project*

- The Project is the area where the movie Timeline resides.
- You grab the Clips from the Event area and place them on that Timeline.
- You edit the Clips on the Timeline by trimming them, using effects and other creative tools.
- You export the finished Timeline (your movie) to a new quicktime movie or other destinations.

Multiple Events - Multiple Projects

- Inside FCPx you can create multiple Events in the Event area based on the way you like to organize your source media (Clips), i.e. different occasions, different locations, different days.
- Inside FCPx you can create multiple Projects for different movies, alternate versions or different reels.
- Both, Events and Projects, are independent modules inside FCPx and the only connection is: Which Clips (from which Event) are used in what Project. Any Clip from any Event can be used in any Project, as long as they are available.
- And remember, there is no need to save any Event or save any Projects. Whatever you work on inside FCPx, every little trim will be automatically saved and next time you re-launch FCPx, everything will be right there.

Basic Concept / Workflow

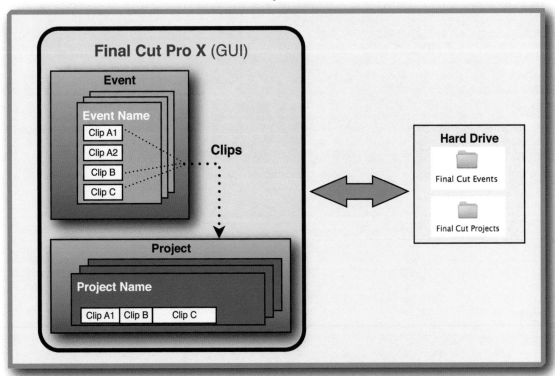

Let's look at one more aspect in this general introduction chapter, the new user interface in FCPx.

Single Window Interface

This single window interface is another major difference in FCPx when compared to FCP7. Many applications nowadays use this interface method:

- ◉ The application, mostly non Document-based, is represented by only one main window.
- ◉ This main window is divided into "Window Panes". These are sections or areas of the window that are always visible or can be displayed or hidden when needed.
- ◉ There are only a few exceptions where some windows can be displayed as separate (mostly) floating windows.

The single window of FCPx is made of 3 main window panes that are always visible and connected. These are the two main elements in FCPx we just discussed, the *Event* and the *Browser*, plus the *Viewer*.

❶ **Event:** Contains the available Clips.

❷ **Project:** Contains the Timeline(s).

❸ **Viewer**: Lets you view the Clips from the Event and the Project.

❹ **Toolbar**: This is the middle strip above the Project. It is not really a window pane but a fixed window element with various controls and displays.

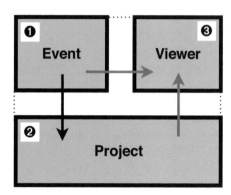

Here is a FCPx screenshot of the main window that displays only the three window panes plus the center Toolbar.

➡ *Resizing*

Any other window pane in FCPx will be shared with one of those main window panes. That window pane keeps its size and won't affect the other two panes. All the resizing is done "inside" the pane. Of course, you can resize the window panes with the divider lines between them. Resizing the main window will resize all window panes proportionally.

➡ *Key Window (key focus)*

When working with multiple windows (separate windows or as part of window panes), it is always important to know which window is the "recipient" of any key stroke from your computer keyboard. That window is called the "*Key Window*" or "*the one that has key focus*". The Key Window is indicated by a little lighter shade of black window background (often hard to see). This is especially important when working with the Inspector.

➡ *Full Screen Mode*

The Full Screen Mode is common in more and more applications, but there are a few details you have to be aware of in FCPx. It offers two Full Screen modes:

Full Screen: Application

Full Screen: Viewer

Exit Full Screen

Window Zoom

☺ **Full Screen Mode for the whole application**

The double arrow in the upper right corner of the main window expands the main window to Full Screen mode and hides the menu bar.

☺ **Full Screen Mode for the Viewer window**

The double Arrow in the lower right corner of the Viewer window pane expands only the Viewer window into Full Screen, hiding everything else. This will automatically start playback.

Moving the mouse into the upper right corner of the computer screen will reveal the blue double arrow to exit Full Screen mode (to press the *Esc* key works only to exit Viewer Full Screen).

☺ **Window Zoom**

This is only "kind of a Full Screen mode". A click on the green window bullet (or Menu command *Window ➤ Zoom*) toggles Window Zoom. This resizes the main window to maximum size without hiding the Menu Bar.

Window Navigation

All the commands to navigate between the window panes and toggle the additional window elements are listed under the Window Menu. Most of the commands are also available as key commands. Please note the difference between the two types of commands.

☺ **Go To a Window Pane**

The *Go To* command switches to a specific window pane. If that window is not visible, it will be made visible first.

☺ **Toggle a Window Pane**

The *Toggle* command switches the visibility of that window. *Show* if it is hidden or *Hide* if it is currently displayed. The current state is displayed in the command (Show ... or Hide...) or with a checkbox next to the command.

Event Viewer

Version 10.0.6 of FCPx added the Event Viewer. This is a second Viewer window that displays only the currently selected Clip in the Event Browser. It has the same identical controls as the main Viewer (except Transform, Crop and Distort).

This window pane is not part of any of the three (always visible) window panes. If selected, it will be inserted between the two main window panes Event and Viewer and resizes both of them depending on the available space.

Here is an overview of all the available window panes on the single FCPx window with their corresponding key commands.

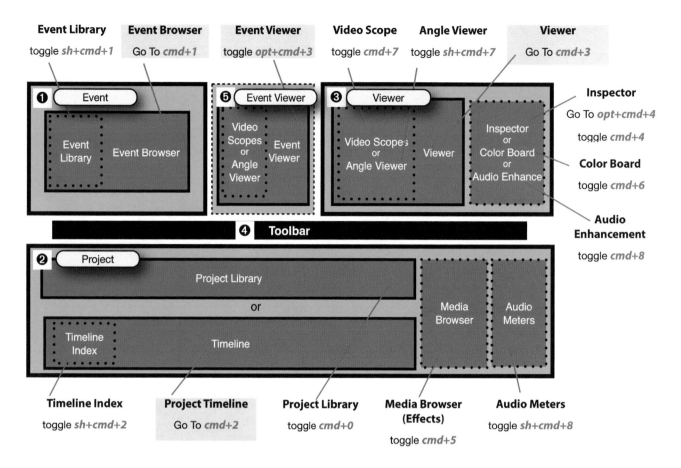

Event Library toggle *sh+cmd+1*

Event Browser Go To *cmd+1*

Event Viewer toggle *opt+cmd+3*

Video Scope toggle *cmd+7*

Angle Viewer toggle *sh+cmd+7*

Viewer Go To *cmd+3*

Inspector Go To *opt+cmd+4* toggle *cmd+4*

Color Board toggle *cmd+6*

Audio Enhancement toggle *cmd+8*

Timeline Index toggle *sh+cmd+2*

Project Timeline Go To *cmd+2*

Project Library toggle *cmd+0*

Media Browser (Effects) toggle *cmd+5*

Audio Meters toggle *sh+cmd+8*

And here is a screenshot where all the window panes are visible as part of the main FCPx main window

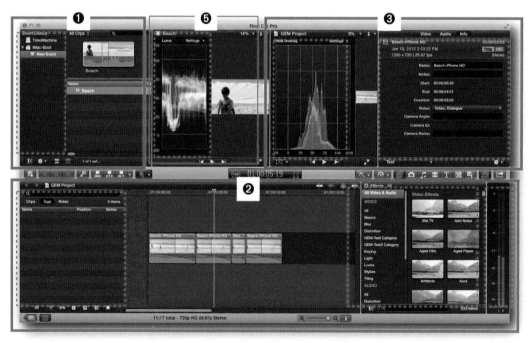

This was just an overview and I will get into the details about each window and its functionality throughout the manuals.

The next step, after understanding the basic concept and user interface in FCPx, is to look at the source material that we use to create our video - the Media Files.

The Source Media Files are the actual building blocks, the raw material, that you use to assemble your video.

Some of the main Media Files are:

- **Video file**: Containing video and sound
- **Audio file**: Containing sound only
- **Image file**: Containing still image only

VideoFile.mov

AudioFile.aif

GraphicsFile.jpg

The Three Incarnations

A Media File exists actually in three "incarnations" when working with FCPx. It is very important to understand their relationship and their function in FCPx.

While the Source Media File is the actual file on your drive, the Event Clip and Timeline Clip, on the other hand, are elements inside FCPx that just represent the Source Media File.

Here is a simple diagram that shows where each of the three incarnation (the Media Files, the Event Clips and the Timeline Clips) "belong" to in the FCPx eco-system.

- **Source Media File**: Finder
- **Event Clip**: FCPx Event Browser
- **Timeline Clip**: FCPx Project Timeline

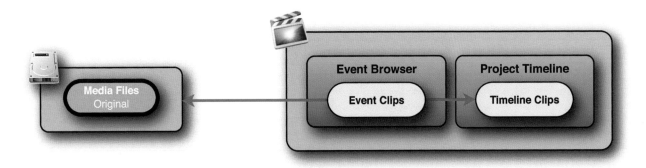

❶ Hard Drive (Finder) ⟫ Media Files

The Media Files have to be stored somewhere on your drive (or camera) so FCPx can access them for the initial import process. When you "import" files into FCPx, it creates only a reference to those files by storing their file path. All the work you do to the files are "non-destructive" edits which means, FCPx NEVER alters the original file on the disk.

> As you can see, it is important NOT to move a Media File after you import it in FCPx; otherwise there will be a broken link and FCPx can't find the file.

❷ Event Browser ⟫ Event Clips (and Subclips)

In order to use Media Files in FCPx, you have to import the files into an Event in FCPx first. When you import a file, FCPx creates a "Clip" that is a representation of the original Media File. All the imported Clips that are listed in the "Event Browser" only contain the path to their file's location on the drive. Whenever you play the "Clip" in the Event Browser, FCPx actually plays back that original Media File it is linked to. The Event Browser functions as a container, holding all the Clips that are available for the Project Timeline.

The Clip stores not only the path to its related Media File but also all its Properties (format, length, etc). You can also add other information to the Clip (tags, informations) to better manage the Clips.

The Clips in the Event Browser are also called *Event Clips*. Subclips are sub-sections of an Event Clip.

❸ Project Timeline ⟫ Timeline Clips

All The Event Clips in the Event Browser now become the source material (building blocks) for your video that you want to create. That video is created on the Project Timeline.

By dragging an Event Clip from the Event Browser to the Project Timeline, you actually create a new Clip, the Timeline Clip, which is a reference to the Event Clip. Although the Timeline Clip is linked to the Event Clip (which is linked itself to the Media File on the disk), it contains its own set of additional properties, i.e. play only the last 5 seconds of the Event Clip, or play back the Clip in black and white or twice as fast, etc.

> As you can see, it is important NOT to remove a Clip from the Event Browser once it is used in the Project Timeline; otherwise, there will be a broken link and FCPx can't find the file.

Properties

Each Media File has specific properties (parameters, characteristics, etc). A video file, for example, has a specific format, sample rate and native resolution. An audio file has a specific format, sample rate and bit depth or embedded metadata like artist, composer, genre, etc.

Not only the Media File itself, but each of the three "incarnations" (**Media File - Event Clip - Timeline Clip**) has their independent properties. I just mentioned that playing an Event Clip or a Timeline Clip is just an instruction to actually play back its linked Media File (let's leave out Rendered Files for the moment). The individual properties of the Clips act as layers that overwrite the original playback properties of the Media File with the properties from the Clip during playback. The instruction from the Clip could be:

- "Play back the Media File, but at half the speed"
- "Play back the Media file in black and white and lower the audio by 6dB"

The following diagram illustrates the connection between **Media File** - **Event Clip** and **Timeline Clip** in regards to their properties:

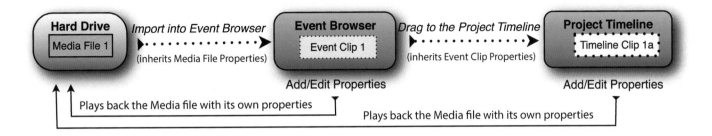

Media File

When you play back a Media File with the Finder's QuickView, it will play that file based on its original properties.

Event Clip

When you import a Media File, FCPx creates an Event Clip and inherits the properties of the Media File. The Inspector (an additional window pane in FCPx) displays those properties.

> FCPx lets you change those properties in the Inspector and even add additional properties to that Event Clip. Please keep in mind that those changed or added parameters are now the properties of the Event Clip and are stored within the Event Clip that FCPx creates. The original Media File on the drive is not altered. The purpose for those additional properties is mainly to manage and organize the Event Clips so you can search and find a specific Clip later among hundreds or maybe thousands of Event Clips in the Event Browser. Some of those Properties could be:
>
> - Additional Text info: Reel No, Scene Number, Date, Location
> - Tags: Ratings, Markers
> - Keywords: Descriptive words or phrases
> - Analyzed Data (automatically performed by FCPx): Excessive shake, how many people in the shot, etc.

Timeline Clips

When you drag an Event Clip (or a portion of it, called a Subclip) from the Event Browser onto the Project Timeline, a Timeline Clip will be created that inherits all the properties of the Event Clip at the time of the "dragging". When you open the Inspector for that new Timeline Clip, you will see those same parameters.

> But now you can apply all kinds of visual or audio changes to the Clip by adding Effects to that Timeline Clip. Please note that those changes will affect only that specific Timeline Clip on the Timeline and not the Event Clip or even the original Media Files. And again, all the parameters are just non-destructive playback parameters.

Reveal in Finder - in Event Browser

You can find out the parent Media File or parent Event Clip.

- ► Select an Event Clip and use any of the commands:
    - Shortcut Menu *Reveal in Finder*
    - Key Command *sh+cmd+R*
- ► Select a Timeline Clip and use any of the commands:
    - Shortcut Menu *Reveal in Event Browser*
    - Key Command *sh+F* (-> Event Browser)
    - Key Command *sh+cmd+R* (-> Finder)

Inspector

The concept of an Inspector is used in many applications. You select an object inside the app (word processor, graphics app) and the Inspector window displays the properties (parameters) of that object and lets you change those parameters.

FCPx uses the same concept. You can open the Inspector window in FCPx as part of the single window UI with the key command *cmd+4* or the Inspector button on the Toolbar 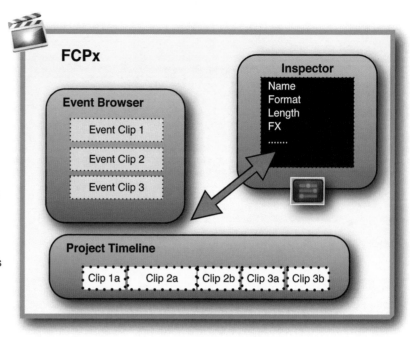. Now when you select an Event Clip or Timeline Clip (or even the Project itself), the window will:

► ... display the properties of the selected Clip.

► ... let you make changes to the properties of the selected Clip.

► You can even select multiple Clips. The Inspector will then indicate if a specific parameter is different between the selected Clips.

The Inspector changes its tabs and the content of the tabs depending on what object is selected:

◉ **Info** contains the main file info, read-only Metadata and additional writable fields. You can even create your own customized fields. And of course you can search for those fields like in a mini database.

◉ **Audio** contains all the audio related properties. All the applied audio FX will be listed here and can be edited. Each individual FX module can be bypassed.

◉ **Video** contains all the video related properties. All the applied video FX will be listed here and can be edited. Each individual FX module can be bypassed.

◉ **Share** lets you apply a collection of Attributes that will be added to the exported file when you share a Project or Clip.

Inspector Tabs

Other Objects like Titles or the Project have different tabs and parameters but the concept is basically the same.

Import to Events

As we saw earlier, the first step when creating a video is to import the Media Files into FCPx, into an **Event,** to be specific.

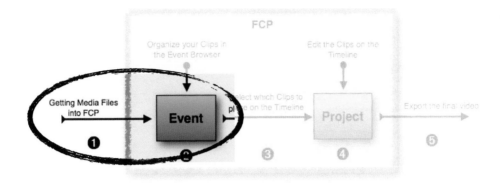

This is the new rule now:

> ### Media Files <u>have to</u> be imported into an Event

This is one fundamental difference to earlier versions of FCP where you could just drag files into a bin and move the Clips around.

FCPx is much more restricted. Every Source Media File has to belong to a specific Event which is like a container of Clips. There cannot be a single Clip in FCPx that is not assigned to an Event. You can, however, create different Events, move Clips between them or import the same Media File to multiple Events.

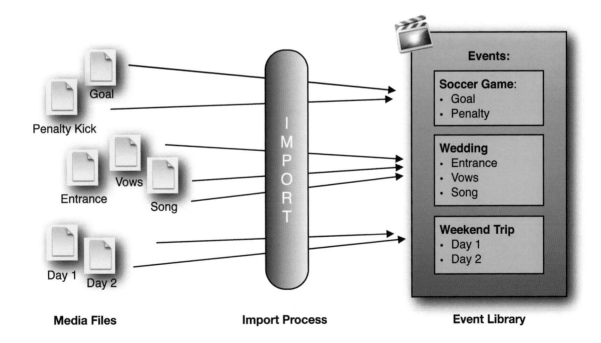

Media Files   **Import Process**   **Event Library**

Based on the fundamental role of the Event in FCPx, it has been assigned its own window pane, one of the three main window panes that are always visible in FCPx's single window GUI; the other two panes are *Project* and *Viewer*.

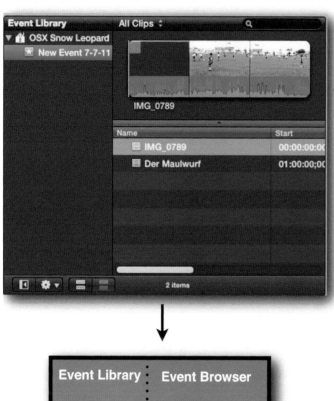

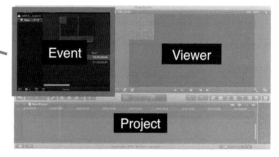

The upper left pane of the single window GUI is the Event pane that is always visible.

The Event pane can be placed on a second connected screen. You can assign a Key Command for that or use the command from the Main Menu:
Window ➤ Show Events on Second Display

To put it back, use
Window ➤ Show Events in the Main Window

The Event Pane has three sections:

🔘 **Event Library**
Lists all the available Events that FCPx can find in its pre-defined locations. This section can be hidden.

🔘 **Event Browser**
Lists all the Clips from the Event(s) that are selected in the Event Library. The Event Browser can be toggled between two views:

- **Filmstrip View**: This is similar to the Finder's Icon View. Every Clip is displayed as an individual film strip made of thumbnail images.

- **List View**: This is actually a combination of List and Icon View, similar to Cover Flow where you have a List View and whatever item is selected in the list will be displayed on top of the list as a Thumbnail Clip.

🔘 **Event Toolbar**
Displays various buttons to manage the Events and their Clips.

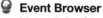

Filmstrip View   List View

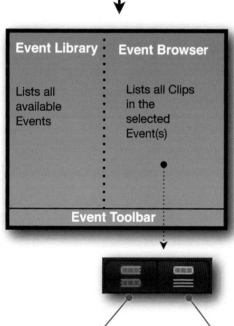

The Event Pane provides a lot of pop-up menus and Shortcut menus (opened by *ctr+click* on the specific item or window background).

The view below is an example for a very simple setup with only one Event that contains two Clips. When working with more Events and Clips and the introduction of Metadata, the interface gets more complex but also more powerful.

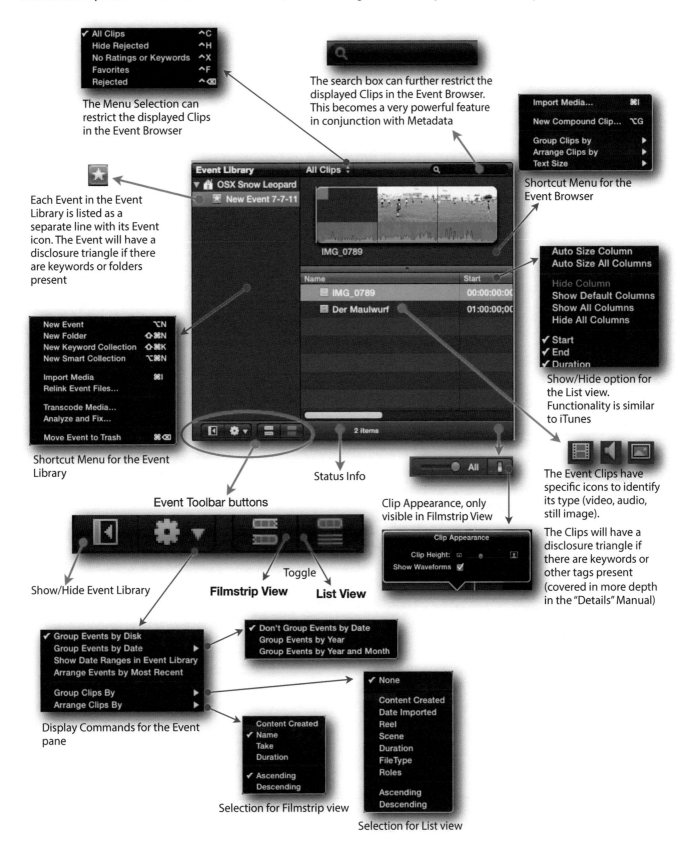

The Menu Selection can restrict the displayed Clips in the Event Browser

The search box can further restrict the displayed Clips in the Event Browser. This becomes a very powerful feature in conjunction with Metadata

Shortcut Menu for the Event Browser

Each Event in the Event Library is listed as a separate line with its Event icon. The Event will have a disclosure triangle if there are keywords or folders present

Show/Hide option for the List view. Functionality is similar to iTunes

Shortcut Menu for the Event Library

Event Toolbar buttons

Status Info

Clip Appearance, only visible in Filmstrip View

The Event Clips have specific icons to identify its type (video, audio, still image).

The Clips will have a disclosure triangle if there are keywords or other tags present (covered in more depth in the "Details" Manual)

Show/Hide Event Library

Filmstrip View **List View**

Toggle

Display Commands for the Event pane

Selection for Filmstrip view

Selection for List view

Event Management

Here are the basic rules for the Event Library:

► All the Events that FCPx can "see" in its dedicated folders on the connected drives are listed in the Event Library.

► You cannot create subfolders for Events to organize them. Not in the Event and not in the "*Final Cut Events*" folder. It is a "flat" list.

► There is only a limited sorting option available to display the Events in the Event Library in subfolders by year and month or by drive.

► The Event itself can contain two kinds of Collections (Keyword Collections and Smart Collections) and also Folders. A disclosure triangle can show/hide those. Please note that these are folders to place Collections in it, not Events.

► Folders (inside an Event) can be created manually to organize Collections.

► Collections and Folders can be moved around (create nested folders) and even copied to different Events (drag-and-drop).

Although the Events are very restricted, there are a variety of commands in the File Menu to manage Events. Any change to the Event in the Event Library will also change the Event Folder and its content on the drive.
Because the listed Events in the Event Library are a representation of an actual folder with the same name in the "*Final Cut Events*" directory, you could do some Event "management" directly in the Finder - if you are brave and know what you are doing. Otherwise, stick to the following commands:

🕯 Duplicate Event...
Make a duplicate of the Event (for easy backup). A Dialog Window gives you the option to name it and select the drive location (if another drive is mounted). Same as *opt+drag* to a new drive in the Event Library.

🕯 Move Event...
Only possible if another drive is mounted to be used as a target disk. A Dialog Window lets you select the new drive.
Same as *cmd+drag* to a new drive in the Event Library.

🕯 Merge Events...
Select two or more Events in the Event Library and choose that command to merge them together into a new Event. You can also *drag* one or many Events onto another Event in the Event Library to merge them together.

🕯 Delete Event Render Files...
A dialog window lets you choose between "All Render Files" or "Unused Render Files Only".

🕯 Organize Event Files...
This command copies all the Source Media Files into the Event folder that had only Alias files there before. This is important to avoid potential broken links with Media Files that are located outside the Event folder.

🕯 Move Event to Trash
This removes the Event from the Event Library and moves the actual Event Folder into the Finder's Trash bin.

Copy Event Clips between Events

You can also copy individual Event Clips between Events. Just *drag* an Event Clip from the Event Browser to a different Event in the Event Library.

Reveal in Finder

This command is available from the Shortcut Menu of each Clip. It opens the Event folder in the Finder to display the Source Media File. If it is an Alias file, then FCPx displays its parent file in its actual location.

Version 10.0.6 of FCPx introduced a new workflow for importing media files. Instead of handling cameras and hard drives as different sources with their own import procedures, everything is now simplified with a single-window interface.

Overview

All the Import options are listed in the Main Menu *File* ➤ *Import*

Main Menu: File ➤ Import

❶ Media...   ⌘I
❷ iMovie Project...
  iMovie Event Library
  Reimport from Camera/Archive... ❹
❸ XML...

❶ **Import Media**

This is the main import option.

❷ **Import iMovie (Project, Library)**

This option lets you import all the Media Files from an iMovie Event Library or the complete iMovie Project with all its Media Files.

❸ **Import XML**

This is a special import option that lets you import files that were encoded as an XML (Extensive Markup Language) file.

❹ **Re-Import missing Media**

This is an import option that lets you re-import previously imported media files that FCPx can't locate. Maybe they are missing, moved or got corrupted.

In this chapter, I cover only the main option, importing Media Files.

Import Media

Whenever dealing with the import of Media Files, keep in mind that there are two different procedures.

Media Import window

➡ *Media Import window*

Import Media File(s) through the Media Import window.

➡ *Drag-and-Drop*

Import Media File(s) directly with drag-and-drop. There are two variations:

- 🔵 **Finder**: Import Media Files by dragging them directly from the Finder onto the open FCPx window.

- 🔵 **Media Browser**: Import Media Files from inside FCPx with drag-and-drop, using the built-in Media Browser.

Media Browser buttons

Import Procedure

➡ *Media Import window*

Here is a basic overview of the steps for the import procedure when using the Media Import window.

Media Import window

Import What
- Any Media File that is stored on a mounted drive or memory card
- Any Media File that is stored on a connected Camera (file-based camera or tape-based camera)
- An "Archive File". This is a special type of camera import, a file that FCPx creates

Import Commands
- File ➤ Import ➤ Media
- *Cmd+I*
- Click Import button on the Toolbar
- Create a new Event and click the "Import Media" button in the Event Browser
- Use the "*Import Media*" command from the Event Browser Shortcut Menu

Media Import Window

Import Settings Sheet

➡ *Drag-and-Drop*

And here is a basic overview of the steps for the import procedure when using drag-and-drop.

Please note that the drag-and-drop import procedure doesn't prompt the Import Settings window.
However, the *Preferences ➤ Import* window in FCPx provides exactly the same settings with the same checkboxes and those settings are automatically applied to every drag-and-drop import in the background.

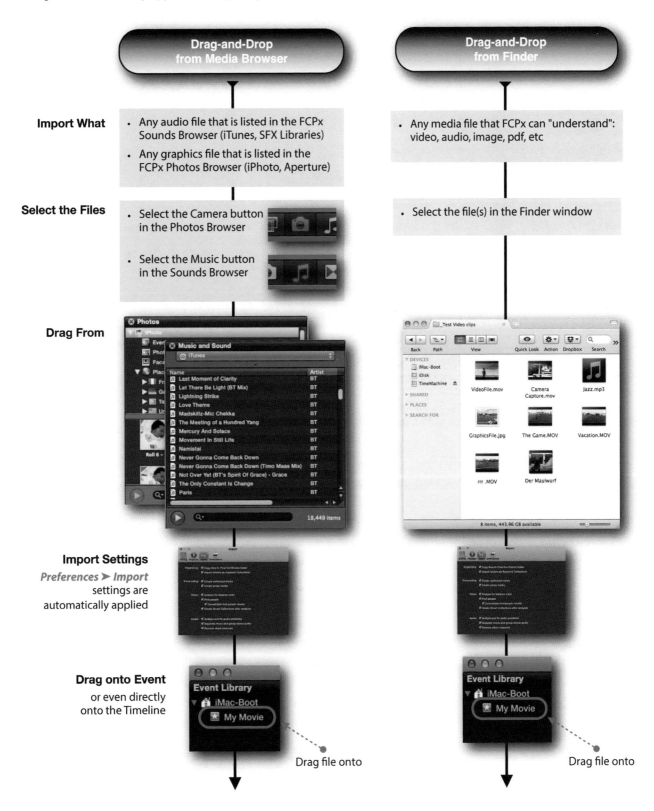

Import Settings

Media Import window

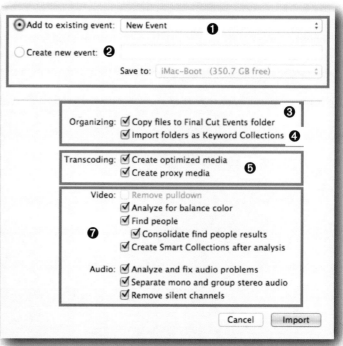

➡ *Assign an Event*

As we have seen before, FCPx demands that every Media File is assigned to (at least) one Event. That means, before we hit the Import button, we have to tell FCPx to which existing Event we want to assign the imported media ❶ or we have to create a new Event ❷ right there. No way around that.

➡ *Create an Event Folder (optional)*

If we create a new Event, FCPx will also create a new folder with the same name in the "Final Cut Events" folder inside the user's Movies directory on your drive. All the files that are related to that Event are stored in that folder.

~/Movies/Final Cut Events/"My Movie"/

➡ *Copy the Source File*

FCPx now creates an "Original Media" folder on your drive inside the Event folder. This is the location where it copies the Media Files. During the File Import you have a checkbox ❸ in the Import window where you can check that procedure. If you leave it unchecked, FCPx will only create an Alias of the Source file in the "Original Media" folder, leaving the Source file at its original location.

An Alias file won't increase the size of your Event folder with additional copies but it is dangerous if you delete the original file later not knowing that it was used in an FCPx Event. (You can replace the alias file with its original file later).

The second checkbox "*Import folders as Keyword Collections* ❹," assigns Keywords to the Clips when you import a folder with Clips (even a nested folder). FCPx keeps that "organizational information" by creating a Keyword for each folder name. That Keyword is a representation of the file's parent folder name. For each Keyword, FCPx will create also a Keyword Collection in the Event Library. The media files will be copied "flat" into the Events folder, all in that one folder without any nested folder! More on Keywords and Keyword Collection in the "Details" book.

➡ *Create an Event Clip*

As we have seen in a previous chapter about the three incarnations of Media Files, FCPx creates an Event Clip during the import that is a representation of the Source Media File. That Event Clip lives inside the Event, now with its own properties.

➡ *Perform Transcoding*

FCPx is resolution independent. You can mix and match different audio and video formats and it transcodes them on the fly.

To optimize the performance, FCPx can use up to 3 different versions of a single Clip. When playing back the Clip in FCPx, it can use the:

- **Original Media** File: That's the original file that gets copied into the Event Folder during the import process.
- **Optimized Media** File: This is a high resolution Apple ProRes format for smoother operations.
- **Proxy Media** File: A low resolution Apple ProRes format for less demanding CPU operations and smaller file size.

The two extra transcoded copies of the original file can be created during the import process by checking their checkboxes ❺. Keep in mind that these files can get quite big. You also can do the transcoding process later.

In the FCPx Preferences window ❻ you can set which one of the three Media files is actually used during playback in FCPx.

➡ *Perform Analysis*

FCPx can analyze the Media Files during the import (it can also be initiated later at any time).

It analyzes the Video and the Audio portion ❼ of the file and makes that data available in two ways:

- **Keywords**: FCPx can store Keywords along with the Event Clip. The Keywords can be searched for later to quickly preview Subclips that match those keywords. For example:
  - Show only the portions of a Clip that has one or two people in the shot
  - Don't show Clips with excessive camera shakes.
- **Settings**: FCPx can detect possible problems and provide settings that can be activated later in the Timeline to help fix those issues. (Again, everything is non-destructive, playback only). For example:
  - Reduce background noise
  - Remove audio tracks that carry no signals.

➡ *Where is all the stuff?*

As we discussed earlier, every Event refers to its own folder inside the *"Final Cut Events"* folder on your drive. The name of the folder inherits the name that you give the Event and when you rename the Event in FCPx, it will automatically rename that folder in the Finder.

The Event Browser displays the content of that Event folder.

Everything that relates to the Event will also be stored inside the Event folder and FCPx expects to find its files exactly where it puts them with exactly the name it gave them. So don't mess with that folder content in the Finder unless you know exactly what you are doing.

All the files that were created during the import can be found here in the Event folder.

- **Final Cut Events** contains a folder for each Event
  - "**My Video**" the name of my Event.
    - **CurrentVersion.fcpevent**: This is the main file that contains the data for the Event (kind of the Project File).
    - **Original Media**: The folder that contains the imported Media Files or the Alias Files linking to the original Media Files.
    - **Transcoded Media:** Contains two subfolders with the transcoded version of the Media Files:
      - **High Quality Media:** Contains the high resolution version.
      - **Proxy Media**: Contains the low resolution version.
    - **Analysis Files**: Contains subfolders that group the analyzed data:
      - **Color Adjustment Files**
      - **Find People Files**
    - **Render Files** contains more subfolders with rendered files.
    - Any other Event-related data.

The *Final Cut Events* folder will automatically be stored in the following directories:

- ▶ On the Boot Drive: In the user's Movies folder "*~/Movies/Final Cut Events/*"
- ▶ On any other Mounted Drive: In its root directory "*/Final Cut Events/*"
- ▶ On a SAN in any directory

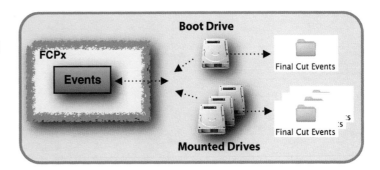

Import Comparison

Here is an overview of all three import options for Media Files.

Although you can drag-and-drop a file directly onto the Project Timeline without importing it first, FCPx still performs the proper import procedure in the background based on the Import Preferences settings (*Preferences*➤*Import*) and also creates the Event Clip in the Event Browser, establishing the proper Event-Project link for that Clip.

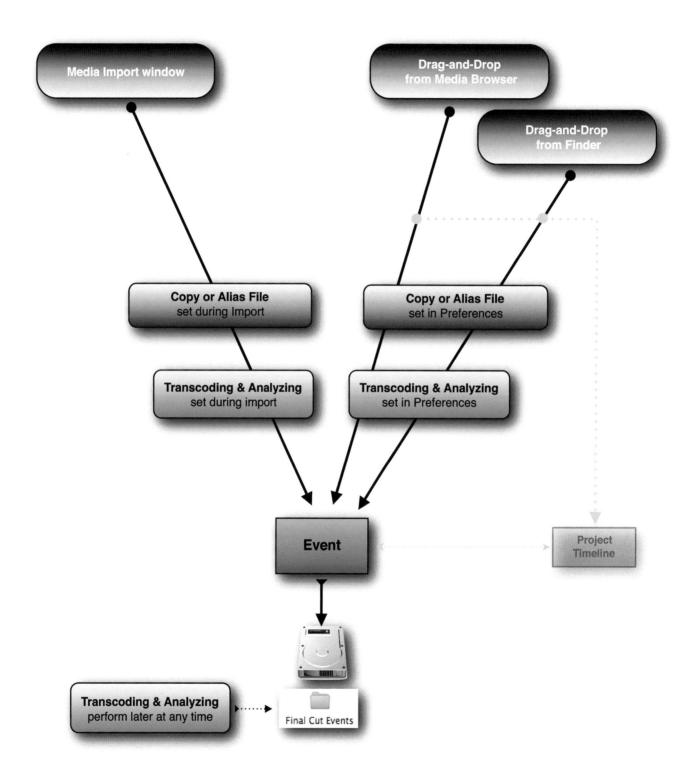

Camera Archives

FCPx provides one special type of import for Cameras that is different from the standard import.

Standard Import vs Archived Import

Standard Import

As we have just seen, these are the steps during a regular import.

- ☑ FCPx stores the imported files on the hard drive in the dedicated "Final Cut Events" folder,
- ☑ It creates Event Clips from those files.
- ☑ It adds the Event Clips to the selected Event in the Event Browser.

Archived Import

An Archived Import functions differently. FCPx acts now as a pure capture utility to get the footage/files off the camera for later use. No clips will be created and nothing will be added to the Event Browser. These are the step:

- ☑ FCPx captures and stores all the imported media files in a special Archive file ❶ with the extension *.fcarch* and a silver reel icon.
- ☑ You can give the Archive file a name and select the destination ❷ (to which mounted drive?), where to store the Archive file.
- ☑ The Archive file is stored on the selected hard drive in the dedicated folder "Final Cut Camera Archives" ❸ that FCPx creates once you create your first Archived import. The folder is placed in the same directory as the "Final Cut Events" folder.
- ☑ An Archive file is actually a Package file that you can open in the Finder (Show Package Content).

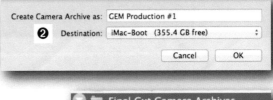

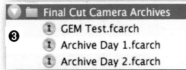

Media Import window

- ▶ The Media Import window is the place where you create an Archive File (store Media Files inside an Archive File) with the "Create Archive..." command.
- ▶ The Media Import window is also the place where you later import (extract) those Media Files from an Archive File into an Event in FCPx.

Media Import window

Now let's have a closer look at the Media Import window. First, these are the commands that open the window:

- Main Menu *File ➤ Import ➤ Media...*
- Key Command *cmd+I*
- *Click* on the Import Media button  on the Toolbar
- Shortcut Menu on the Event Library *Import Media*
- Selecting an empty Event in the Event Library will display the "Import Media" button in the Event Browser

Toolbar

Empty Event

The Media Import window is divided into five main sections. The look and availability of Section 2-4 depends on the selected item. The sections can be resized by dragging their divider lines.

❶ **Sidebar**: All the available sources on your computer, from where you can import Media Files, are listed here, grouped together by categories: Cameras - Devices - Camera Archives - Favorites

❷ **Browser**: This section lets you browse the content (files) of the selected item in the Sidebar.

❸ **Filmstrip**: This section is optional and is only displayed if the selected item is a video file.

❹ **Viewer**: This section is the Viewer of the selected item. It might have additional playback controls if the selected item is a video file.

❺ **Commands**: On the bottom of the window are the buttons for the import commands.

Media Import window

Now let's have a closer look at each section and their functionality.

Sidebar

The sidebar looks and functions similarly to the Finder's sidebar or the sidebar in iTunes. Here it lists all the possible sources from where you can import Media Files. Those sources are grouped into four sections.

➡ Cameras

Any camera, tape-based or file-based, that is connected to your computer is listed in this sections, including the built-in iSight camera on your computer.

➡ Devices

This section lists all the mounted storage devices. These include.

- 🔘 Mounted local drives
- 🔘 Mounted network drives
- 🔘 Mounted (inserted) memory cards

➡ Camera Archives

This section lists all the available Camera Archives.

➡ Favorites

This section is not an additional source of possible Media Files. If you have folder(s) on your mounted drives that you often access for importing media, then you can *drag* those folders (from the content area) onto this section (drag over the word "Favorites"). That folder will now be listed in this Favorites section and lets you quickly select it without drilling down in the folder structure from a selected Device. Drag any location off the sidebar to remove it from the list.

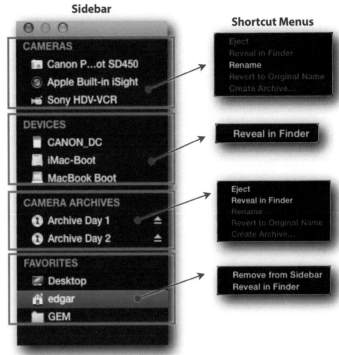

Content - Filmstrip - Viewer

While the appearance of the sidebar on the left doesn't change much, the right side of the Media Import window is highly dynamic. Its appearance depends on what item is selected in the Sidebar and then what specific file is selected.

The default is *List View* but some selections allow to switch to *Filmstrip View*. The selection goes from bottom to the top. That means, what is selected at the bottom is displayed in the section above.

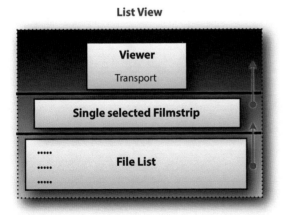

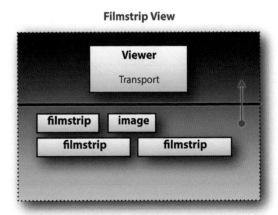

Here are the details about the different Views depending on the selected items in the sidebar.

➡ *Devices*

Selecting any mounted Device from the Sidebar displays all the files ❶ of that directory. This is like List View in the Finder.

- ☺ Whatever media file is selected in the list will be displayed above as a single filmstrip ❷.
- ☺ The file will also be displayed in the Viewer ❸ above.
- ☺ If the selected file is a video file, then the Viewer will display the Playback controls ❹.
- ☺ The single filmstrip in the middle can be "skimmed" ❺ when *dragging* the mouse over it. A Skimmer info tag displays the name and the position of the Clip. The Viewer above follows the skimming position.
- ☺ The switch button ❻ at the lower right corner opens the *Clip Appearance* window which lets you show/hide the waveform in the filmstrip.
- ☺ The Browser lists the items with Metatdata columns that function in a standard way. *Click* a column header to sort the items, move or resize the columns and *ctr+click* on the header to bring up the window to show/hide specific metadata columns ❼.
- ☺ Select a single or multiple files. The standard selection commands apply. *Sh+click* to select contiguous items or *cmd+click* to select (deselect) multiple non-contiguous items. *Cmd+A* selects all items.
- ☺ *Click* the *Import Selected...* or *Import All...* button to pull out Import Settings sheet ❽.
- ☺ Select the setting you want and *click* the Import ❾ button to start the Import process.
- ☺ Please note that you cannot import a range selection of a Clip (Subclip). You can only import entire clips.

Media Import: Devices

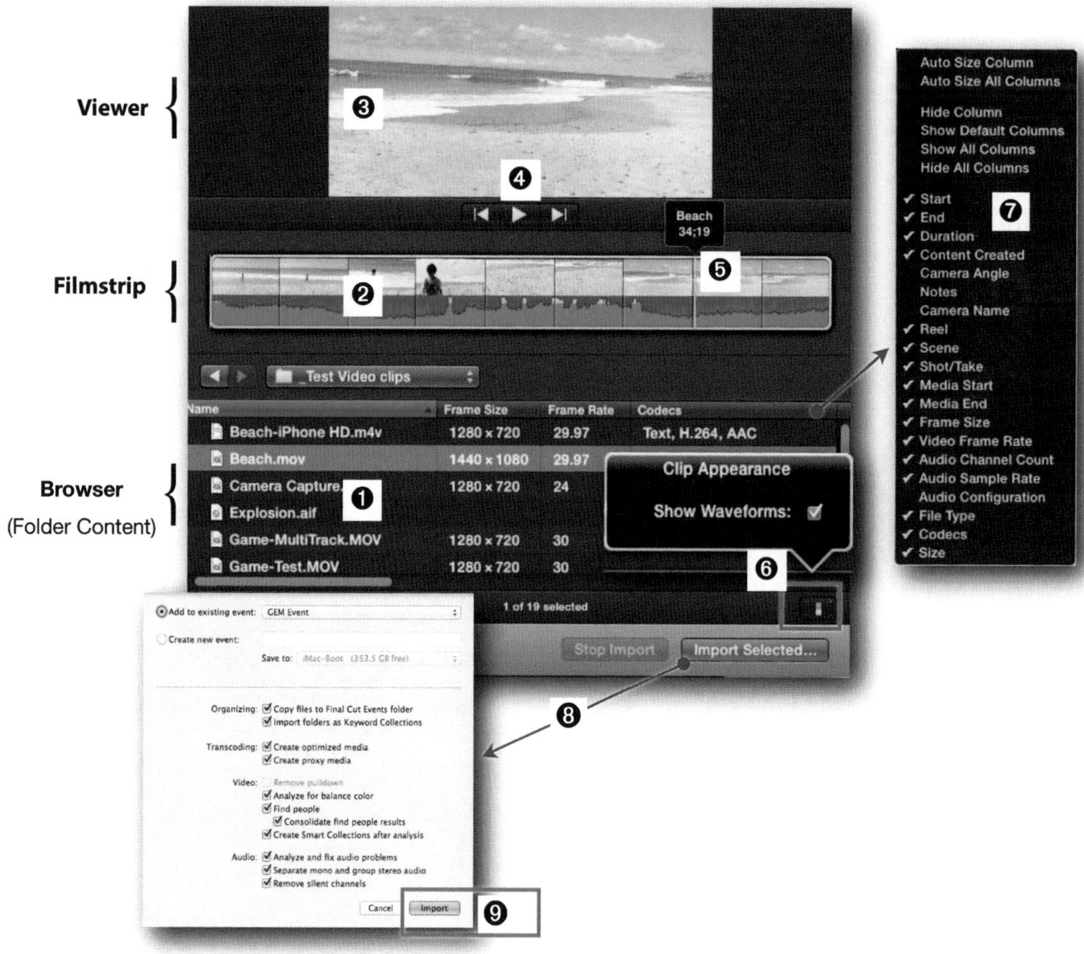

➡ *Archives*

The Media Import window automatically mounts any Archive File on all the mounted drives it can find in their dedicated folder location (indicated by its visible Eject button). *Click* on any unmounted Archive file in the Sidebar to mount it.

Selecting a Camera Archive from the Sidebar displays all the media files that where captured previously in that Archive file.

The content can be displayed in two different Views. The view button ❶ switches between them:

☻ List View

This is the same view we just saw in the view for Devices. It functions the same way.

☻ Filmstrip View

The filmstrip view has only two sections. The lower part displays all the available media files as filmstrips ❷ and the upper part, the Viewer ❸ with the transport controls. The skimming works on all filmstrips the same as with the single filmstrip in List View.

The Switch button opens the Clip Appearance ❹ window that lets you set the Clip Height. The slider ❺ to the left lets you adjust the visible length of the filmstrips.

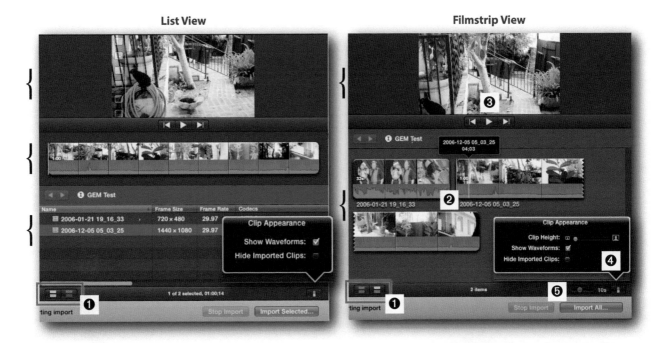

Import Subclips

You can select one or multiple portions of a clip (Subclip) for import. *Drag* (single selection) or *cmd+drag* (multiple selection) on the filmstrip, even selecting portions on different filmstrips. You can switch between List View ❻ and Filmstrip View ❼ without losing the selections.

The selected range is marked with the yellow frame ❽ that you can trim by *cmd+dragging* the left and right border.

Cmd+click directly on a frame deactivates the selection so it will not be included in the import. The visible frame is dimmed ❾. *Cmd+click* again to reactivate it. The selection was not lost.

➡ Camera (file-based)

There are a wide variety of cameras that can be connected to your computer. The view of the Media Import window depends on the type of media you are viewing/importing from a particular camera.

- ▶ File-based Camera
- ▶ Tape-based Camera
- ▶ iSight Camera (live video signal)

Let's look at the file-based Camera type first.

FCPx supports the Picture-Transfer-Protocol (PTP) which lets you display all the files on a connected camera directly in the Media Import window where you can select and import them. The files can be displayed in two different Views. The view button ❶ switches between them:

☻ List View

This is the same view we just saw in the view for Devices. It functions the same way.

☻ Filmstrip View

The filmstrip view again has only two sections. The lower part displays all the available media files as filmstrips ❷ and the upper part, the Viewer ❸ with the transport controls. The skimming works on all filmstrips the same as with the single filmstrip in List View.

The Switch button opens the Clip Appearance ❹ window that lets you set the Clip Height. The slider ❺ to the left lets you adjust the visible length of the filmstrips.

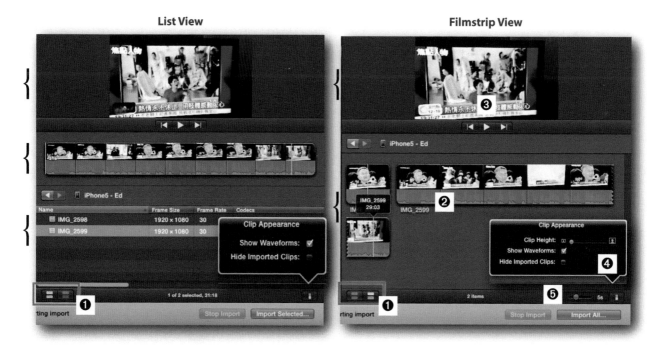

Archive File

Although it is possible to import the files from a camera directly to FCPx and back the files up with your system, it is safer to create a separate Camera Archive first. Those Archive files are easy to move around in the Finder and can be backed up to any other storage device.

To create a Camera Archive

- ☑ Select the files in the Media Import window
- ☑ Click the *Create Archive...* Button at the bottom of the Sidebar.
- ☑ Select a name, a destination and click OK to create the Archive file

➡ Camera (tape-based)

- The Media Import window displays only the Viewer ❶ when connected to a tape-based camera.

- The Playback Controls ❷ at the bottom lets you remote control the camera. The playback status and the timecode will be displayed at the top.

- *Click* the *Import...* ❸ button which opens the Import Settings ❹ sheet to configure the settings for the import.

- *Click* the *Import* ❺ button to start the import from the current tape position.

- *Click* the *Stop Import* ❻ button to stop the import process. This will save the new Media File in the Final Cut Events folder, create an Event Clip from that file and place it in the selected Event in FCPx.

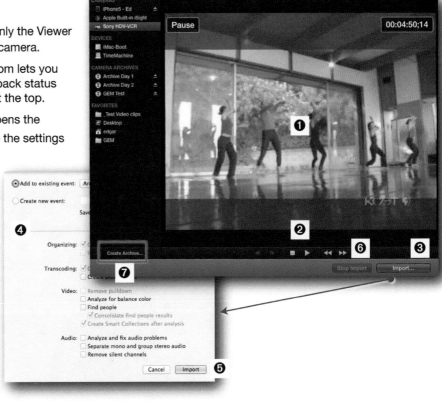

Archive File

Creating an Archive file of the video tape first before importing it into FCPx has several advantages. Besides the additional backup benefits, the import of an Archive File is more flexible.

- ☑ *Click* the *Create Archive...* ❼ button.

- ☑ The tape rewinds automatically and imports from the beginning.

- ☑ You can stop in between to abort the import or keep the footage that is imported so far.

- ☑ The import creates individual Media Files when it detects the different recording sections on tape.

➡ Camera (live)

"Importing" a live video signal from a connected iSight camera or any other camera that outputs a live video signal means that you are "recording" video directly into FCPx.

- ☑ The Media Import window displays only the Viewer, which is the signal from the video camera.

- ☑ *Click* the *Import...* button which opens the Import Settings sheet first.

- ☑ Make the appropriate settings.

- ☑ *Click Import* to start the recording.

- ☑ Press the *Stop Import* button to stop the recording.

Import Settings sheet

Let's review the various settings on the Import Settings sheet that pulls out every time before an import.

❶ Event Assignment

This is the part where FCPx forces you to assign a specific Event for the Media Files that you are about to import.

> ► **Add to existing event:**
> A pop-up menu lists all the existing Events that are currently available in FCPx.

> ► **Create new event:**
> You can create a new Event right here without going back to the Event pane. Enter an Event name and select to which mounted drive you want to save the Event.

❷ Organizing

Check to copy the source file into the Event folders or uncheck to just create an Alias. Check to create Keywords from nested folder names.

Copy files is automatically checked when importing from tape-based Cameras and live-video Cameras

❸ Transcoding

Here you check whether or not you want FCPx to create the two additional files for each original Media File (high res and low res).

Optimized Media is automatically checked when importing from tape-based Cameras and live-video Cameras

❹ Analysis

Here you check whether or not FCPx should analyze the imported files and create and store Keywords and Settings along with the Clip: Shaky video, color balance, excessive hum or loudness, close or wide shot, how many people in the shot, etc.

❺ Import:

A click on this button will perform the file import based on the above settings.

> ☑ FCPx creates the new Event (if selected).

> ☑ FCPx creates an Event Clip for each imported Media File and assigns it to the selected Event.

> ☑ FCPx performs the two transcodings of each Media File (if selected).

> ☑ FCPx performs the Analysis for Video and Audio and stores the Keywords and Settings with the created Event Clips (if selected).

Drag-and-Drop from Media Browser

❶ Select Photos

From the central Toolbar in FCPx select the "Photos" button to open the Photos Browser displaying available Photos.

- You can search your current iPhoto Library right inside FCPx.
- You can search your current Aperture Library right inside FCPx.

❷ Select Music or Sound FX

From the central Toolbar select the "Music" button to open the Media Browser displaying available Music and Sound files.

- You can search and preview your current iTunes Library.
- You can search and preview any installed sound Libraries (FCPx, Soundtrack).

❸ Drag the File to the Event

To import a photo or audio file to an Event, you just *drag* the file from the Media Browser onto the Event in the Event Library (not the Event Browser!) You can also drag the files directly onto the Timeline.

❹ Import

By dragging a file from the Media Browser onto the Event, FCPx imports the files into the Event based on the "Organizing, Transcoding, Analysis" settings in the *Preferences ➤ Import* window ❺.

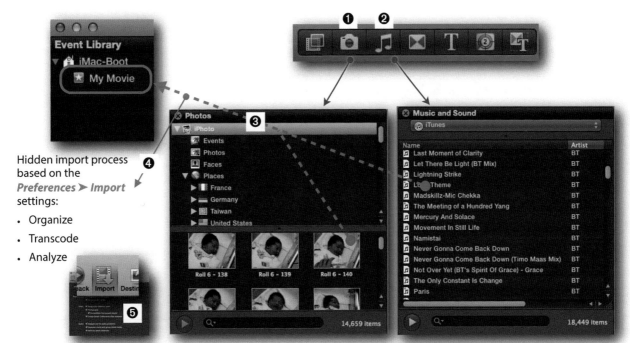

You can search for and preview media files directly in the Media Browser

Drag-and-Drop from Finder

Importing Media File from the Finder is the most simple step of adding files to your FCPx project.

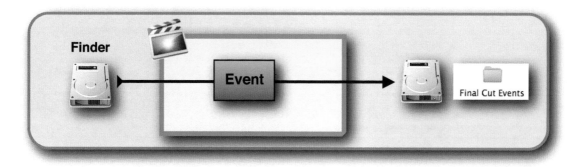

The drag-and-drop from Finder procedure is a fast way to get Media into FCPx from anywhere on your drive(s):

❶ Select any Media File(s) in a Finder window.

❷ *Drag* the file(s) to an existing Event in the FCPx Event Library (you could also drag it directly onto the Timeline).

❸ The import procedure is done "behind the scenes" based on the settings in the *Preferences ➤ Import* window.

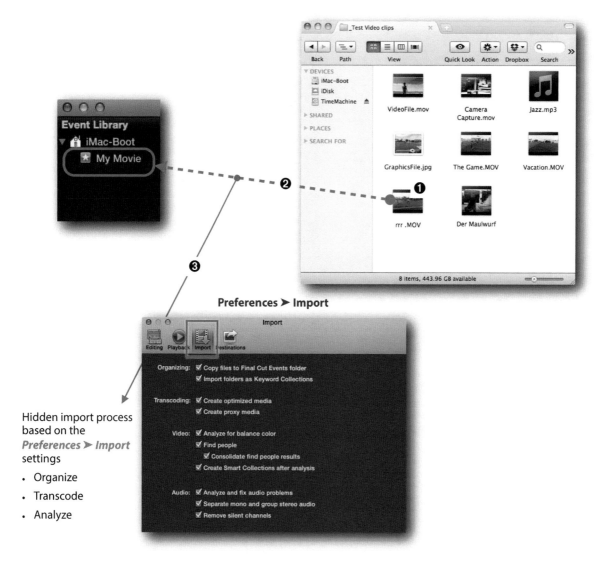

Preferences ➤ Import

Hidden import process based on the *Preferences ➤ Import* settings
- Organize
- Transcode
- Analyze

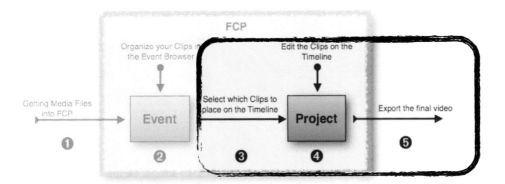

The Concept

Now that we have a basic understanding of the first big component in FCPx, the Event, and how to get media into the Event, let's look at the other component, the *Project*.

The main task of the Event is to collect (import) the media files, organize them and prepare their use in the new video. It provides the source material to create our video. The actual creation however is done in the Project. The main steps are:

- ☑ Grab the chosen Clips from the Event(s) and organize them in sequence on the Timeline.
- ☑ Edit the sequence: Trim the Clips, add effects and other creative treatments.
- ☑ When finished, export the final video as a new quicktime file.

You can work for days or weeks in the Event area creating Events and organizing your Clips without having started on a single Project. Remember, you are collecting Media Files without any concerns about their different formats. Later, when we start with the actual Project, FCPx will conform any frame size, frame rate or sample rate to a unique Render Format that we can choose and even change at any time (with some minor restrictions).

Note: The Project itself doesn't store any Media Files or Aliases of the Media Files (that's the job of the Event).

The Project stores only the reference to each Event Clip in an Event and that Event Clip has a reference to the original Source Media File.

The same way an imported Clip cannot exist without a reference to an Event, a Project too cannot exist without a reference to at least one Event. FCPx won't let you create a Project without a reference to a *Default Event*.

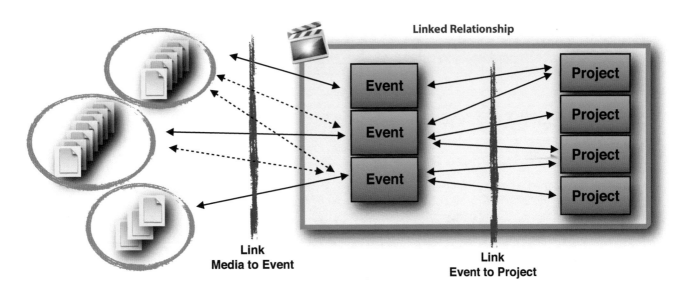

Project GUI

As we know by now, the Project pane is one of the three main window sections in FCPx that is always visible.

While every other window pane has its main sections with additional window elements that can be shown or hidden, the Project pane is different and unique. It has a dual identity, displaying two different views:

- **Project Library**: This one is the first view when no Project has been created yet. It prompts you to create your first Project. That Project and any other Project created later (that FCPx finds in the dedicated "*Final Cut Projects*" folder) will be displayed here.

- **Timeline**: This view is the actual work place where you compile your video. The Timeline View has an optional window element that can be shown/hidden, the *Timeline Index*.

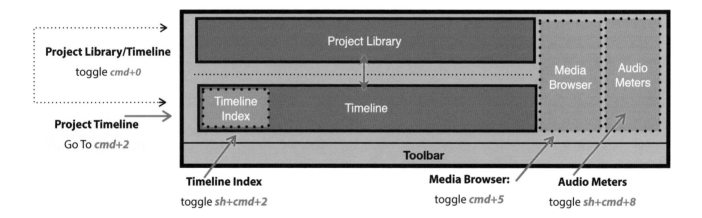

You can toggle between the two Project views with the Key Command *cmd+0* or the film reel button in the lower left corner on the Project's Toolbar strip.

Project Library is displayed: Project Timeline is displayed:

The Media Browser and Audio Meters can be toggled independently from the Project Library and Timeline view.

The Project Toolbar is the Strip at the bottom of the Project pane that displays various buttons, controls and infos depending on the Project Library or Project Timeline view:

Project Toolbar in **Project Library** view

Project Toolbar in **Project Timeline** view   00:00 total - NTSC SD 29.97i Surround

Project Library

It is important to point it out again: Projects cannot be loaded manually into FCPx. FCPx automatically "lists" all the Projects that it can find in pre-defined drive locations, the "*Final Cut Projects*" folder(s). There is also no "Save Project" command. Any changes made in the Project are saved automatically and immediately to various files in its Project folder.

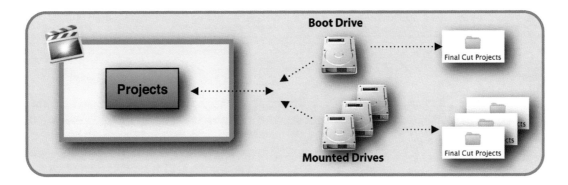

The *Final Cut Projects* folder will automatically be stored in the following directories (if selected):

- ▶ On the Boot Drive: In the user's Movies folder "*~/Movies/Final Cut Projects/*"
- ▶ On any other Mounted Drive: In the root directory "*/Final Cut Projects/*"
- ▶ On a SAN in any directory

Each Project in FCPx is represented by an identical named folder inside the "*Final Cut Projects*" folder or in a nested subfolder. Here is a big difference. Remember that Events can only exist on one level in the Event Library window. Projects on the other hand can be organized in subfolders in the Project Library window,.

The Project Library window in FCPx lists each Project that it can find in any of the *Final Cut Projects* folder as a single filmstrip with a header on the left displaying the Project name, duration, last update and also its relative location inside a drive's *Final Cut Project* folder.

Next to the header is the long single filmstrip displaying the state of the current Project with a series of thumbnail images of that Project. Those filmstrips represent the complete Timeline of each Project. You can skim along the filmstrip by moving the mouse over it and hit the *space* key to start playing the Project from the red skimmer position. Turn Audio Skimming on/off with the Key Command *sh+S* or Menu Command *View ➤ Audio Skimming*.

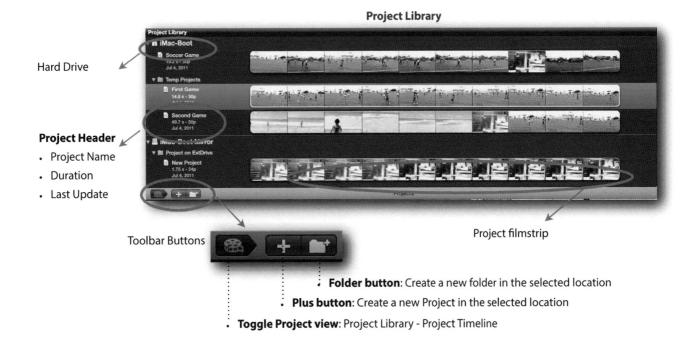

Folder button: Create a new folder in the selected location

Plus button: Create a new Project in the selected location

Toggle Project view: Project Library - Project Timeline

Create a Project

Before we get into the actual video creation on the Timeline, let's have a look at the initial creation of a Project first.

The + button in the Project Library toolbar lets you create a new Project. It is important to select the right hard drive or subfolder in the Project Library first because that will be the location of your new Project (in the browser and on the drive). If you want to place the Project into a subfolder you can create the folder(s) first with the Folder button. However, you can later drag Projects and folders freely around in the Project Library.

When you click the + button, a settings sheet will open up where you set the properties for the new Project. The button in the left lower corner toggles between the two settings views: "*Automatic Settings* ❶" (Stereo, 48kHz, ProRes 422, SMPTE 1:0:0:0) and "*Custom Settings* ❷".

❸ **Name**: This will set the name of the Project and also the name of the Projects folder in the "*Final Cut Projects*" folder on your drive. You can rename the Project later at any time.

❹ **Default Event**: You have to assign at least one Event to the Project called the "*Default Event*". However, you can later use Clips from any other available Event. Those other "used Events" are called "*Referenced Events*".

❺ **Starting Timecode**: Set the SMPTE start time for the Project Timeline.

❻ **Video Properties**: When left at the default setting, FCPx does not set the Project Properties. Later, when you drag your first Event Clip onto the Project Timeline, FCPx looks up the video properties of that first Clip and uses those as the Project Properties. Choosing the *Custom* button expands the window where you can manually set the Format, Resolution and Frame Rate.

❼ **Audio Properties:** You can leave it at the default setting (Stereo, 48k) or choose *Custom* to select from the popup menus.

❽ **Render Properties**: You can leave it at the default settings (Apple ProRes 422) or choose *Custom* to select different settings. This sets the codec for the background rendering of your Project.

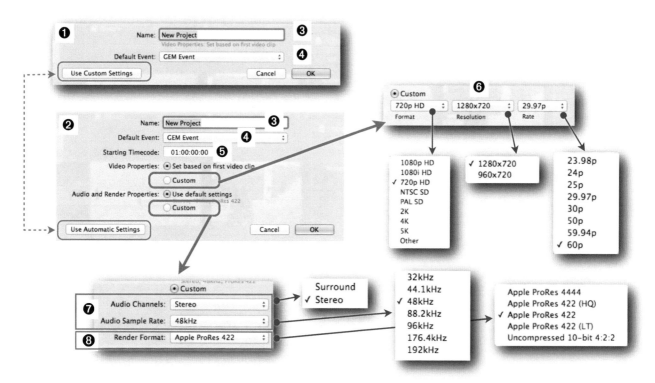

It is a good idea to choose the settings based on the format you plan to use for your final video export. However, all those settings can be changed at any time without a problem, except the video frame rate which could cause your Clips to shift in the Timeline.

Change Project Properties

You can change the Project Properties at any time by selecting the Project in the Project Library and open the Inspector with *cmd+4* or click the Inspector button on the Toolbar .

The *Properties* Tab displays the following info:

- ◉ The Name of the Default Event and the other Project Properties.
- ◉ The *General* section displays the location and the last modification date of the Project and lets you enter some *Notes*.
- ◉ Other Events that are used by this Project are listed under "*Referenced Events*". The button "Modify Event References" opens a settings sheet where you change the order of Events and therefore the priority if you have multiple Events in your Project that link to the same Media File.
- ◉  Wrench (*Project Properties Button*): This button in the lower right corner opens the Projects Properties Settings window with the same parameters that we have seen when we first created a Project. Now you can change all those Project Properties (maybe not the Frame Rate).

Manage Projects

- **Rename** Projects or Folders by *clicking* on their name in the Project Library. This will also rename the corresponding Project folder or nested folder on your drive.
- **Move** Projects or Folders: Just *drag-and-drop* Projects or Folders in the Project Library. This will also move the corresponding Project folder or nested folder on your drive.
- Three more actions are available from the Project Library's Shortcut Menu: *Ctr+click* or select from the File Menu, if Projects have key focus. Keep in mind that the File menu changes its content based on what object or window is selected (Event or Project Library).

    - **Duplicate Project ...** opens a settings sheet (see image below).
    - **Consolidate Project Media ...** opens a settings sheet (see image below).
    - **Move Project to Trash** removes the selected Project or Folder from the Project Library and moves its corresponding files in the Finder to the Trash.

- The File Menu lists the same commands plus three more:

    - **Move Project ...** to a different drive.
    - **Organize Project Files ...** to restart interrupted media management processes.
    - **Delete Project Render Files ...** to save space. They can be re-rendered later again.

Duplicate Projects - Settings

Consolidate Projects Media - Settings

Let's have a look at the Timeline, the center piece of your work where you create your new video. FCPx uses a slightly different approach than other Video Editing software, including its predecessor FCP7.

GUI

The center of the Project Timeline GUI is of course the Timeline where you place the Clips.

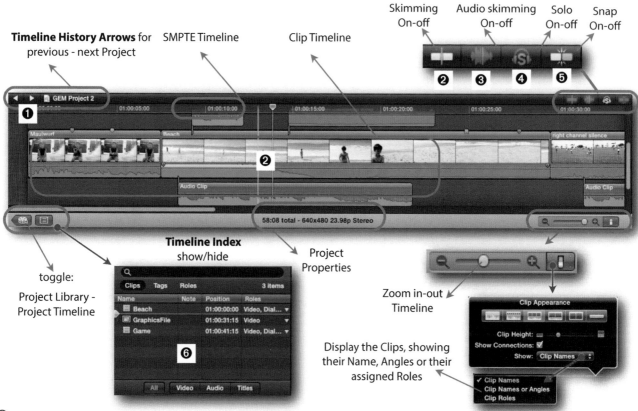

☻ Timeline History

Those arrows ❶ let you quickly switch to the previous or next Project without switching to the Project Library window. You can step only through the Projects that have been selected (kind of "active in the background") after you launch FCPx. The name of the visible Project is displayed next to the arrows.

☻ Skimming

This is a scrubbing feature where you move the mouse over a Clip and the Clip plays back corresponding to the position of your mouse and the speed of your mouse movement. The play position is indicated by a red Skimming Bar on the Clip ❷.

☻ Skimming Audio

This lets you turn off the audio skimming ❸ if you need only a visual reference without the "noise".

☻ Solo

This solos the audio portion ❹ of the selected Clip. Audio from other non-selected Clips is muted.

☻ Snap

When enabled ❺, dragged objects or the Playhead or Skimmer will snap to the nearest object or Playhead.

Timeline Index

The Timeline Index is a window pane ❻ that slides out from the left of the Timeline window. It lists all the Clips used in the displayed Project. Use the filter buttons on the bottom and the search box to restrict the displayed list. Select the "*Tags*" tab to only display the Keywords, Ratings and Markers that are used in the current Clips. Select the "*Roles*" tab for using the powerful Roles feature (see the "Details" manual). The selected item(s) in the list will be indicated in the Timeline with a white border around the Clip's range.

No More Sequences

Prior to FCPx, each Project (the wedding video, your vacation video or your next blockbuster movie) was represented by a document file that you opened, saved, and closed similar to text documents in a word processor. Each project contained all the related media files and you edited your video on a regular Timeline. Each Project could also have multiple Timelines, called Sequences. When you wanted to edit a different version of your project (short version, outtakes, alternatives), you just created a new sequence which gave you a new Timeline for that alternate video edit. Everything stayed with that one Project and when you saved it, all the sequences were saved with it.

FCPx is a totally different story. **One Project - One Timeline**. And there are no Sequences anymore! As we've learned earlier, FCPx automatically displays all the Projects that it currently "sees" on your drive(s). All your available Media Files, organized in Events, are available right there. You are basically working in one big FCPx *"über-Project"*. If you want to start a new Timeline (formerly known as a Sequence) to create an alternate version, you have to create a new Project. One option to imitate the Sequence concept is to organize the Projects in nested folders, but still One Project - One Timeline.

Each Timeline is a Sequence that lives inside a Project

Each single Timeline represents a single Project

Primary Storyline - Connected Clips

And here is another new approach in FCPx: Standard video editor applications work with the concept of tracks on a Timeline. Using that approach, you could create a few video tracks and even more audio tracks to position your video and audio clips on and arrange them in the correct sequence.

But FCPx uses a new approach with a single **Storyline** and **Connected Clips**.

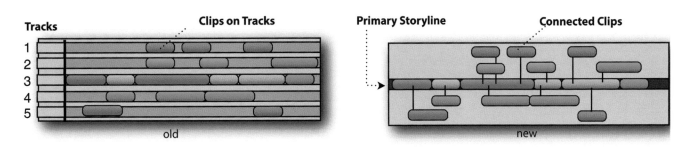

Here are some of the fundamental changes:

- Instead of multiple tracks in the Timeline, there is only one "track", called the **Primary Storyline**.
- There is no distinction anymore between video and audio tracks. They live together identified by their color code.
- Layered Clips are not placed on parallel tracks, they are now "*connected*" to the Clip on the Primary Storyline, becoming **Connected Clips**. When moving a Clip on the Primary Storyline, all its connected Clips move along with it, staying perfectly in sync.
- Video Clips that include audio tracks don't have to be split in their separate video and audio content. They can be treated (placed, moved, trimmed) as one composite Clip. They can be extracted and edited separately if needed.

So Clips don't get placed on tracks. Instead, they "live" in two main areas:

- **On** the Primary Storyline

  It is technically a single track or a main track where you place your Clips.

- **Outside** the Primary Storyline (above or below)

  Any additional Clip, video or audio, is now placed parallel to the storyline, not onto a separate track. This will connect them to the Clip on the main track, the Primary Storyline.

Primary Story Line and Connected Clips

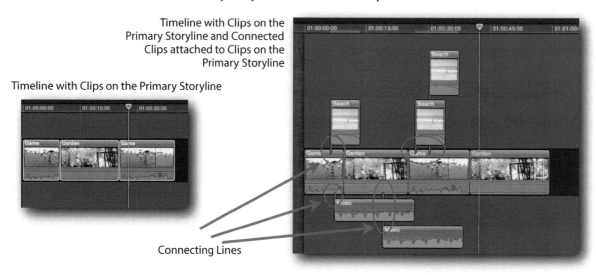

Timeline with Clips on the Primary Storyline and Connected Clips attached to Clips on the Primary Storyline

Timeline with Clips on the Primary Storyline

Connecting Lines

▶ The Connected Clips have a "***Connecting Line***" that shows where they are attached to their parent Clip on the Primary Storyline. That connecting point on the parent Clip will move when you moved the Connected Clip. The connecting point at the Connected Clip always starts at its first frame as a default but can be moved with a *opt+cmd+click* anywhere on the Connected Clip (note, both Clips stay in sync, only the position of the line changes).

▶ When moving a Clip on the Primary Storyline, all the Connected Clips that are attached to it will move with it and stay in sync, a big workflow improvement (with a few hidden dangers).

▶ Connected Clips that overlap will automatically stack on top of each other keeping their connecting line to the main Clip. Visually, everything is moving elegantly out of the way and into place when necessary.

▶ A video clip that has audio tracks embedded can now be treated as a single Clip to better ensure the sync between its video and audio content.

▶ The Clip on the Primary Storyline doesn't have to be a video clip, it can be an audio clip too.

▶ There is a 'top to bottom' priority for video clips. The top video or image Clip blocks any video or image below regardless if they are placed on the Primary Storyline or if they are Connected Clip (different story with transparency).

▶ Audio tracks from audio clips or video clips always mix together when stacked on top of each other.

▶ The Clips on the Primary Storyline have to be attached to each other. There cannot be any gap between Clips like in previous FCP versions. Any potential gap will be automatically closed ("***Magnetic Timeline***") or will be filled with a "*Gap Clip*".

Advanced Timeline Features

There are many other new Timeline features and concepts in FCPx which I cover in my second book *"Final Cut Pro X - The Details"*.

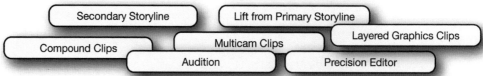

Before getting into the editing procedure, let's understand the Clips a little bit better and the third pane in the GUI that actually lets us view those Clips, the Viewer.

The Viewer

Originally, FCPx had only one Viewer, but since version 10.0.6 it provides a second Viewer called the *Event Viewer*.

Event Viewer	Viewer
Window pane can be added with the command "Show/Hide Event Viewer"	Always visible as part of the three main window panes
Only displays the currently selected Event Clip in the Event Browser	Displays the currently selected Event Clip or the selected Time. If the Event Viewer is visible, then it displays only the Timeline
Provides all the Viewer controls with the exception of Transform, Crop, Distort	Provides all the Viewer controls
Can be viewed in Full Screen Mode	Can be viewed in Full Screen Mode
Both Viewers can be placed together on a second display with the command "Show Viewers on Second Screen"	

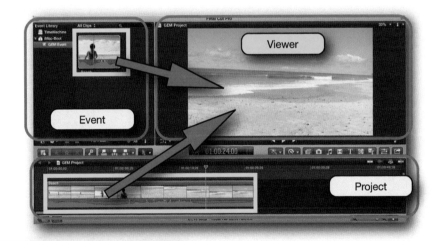

If Event Viewer is hidden

If Event Viewer is visible

What is Playing Where?

When wondering what Clip you're seeing or what Clip is playing in a specific Viewer, you have to be aware of the OSX concept "*Key Window*" or "*the window with key focus*". This is the target window, the recipient, for whatever you type on your computer keyboard, a keyboard shortcut or a text input.

◉ Viewer only

If only the Viewer is visible, then it displays the Event or the Project, whichever has key focus (the currently selected window). The Start command *space bar* will play back either the currently selected Clip if the Event has key focus, or the Timeline of the selected Project (regardless of what Clip is selected on the Timeline) if the Project has key focus. The Viewer Title with its icon in the upper left corner indicates which one is currently selected, or which one is "feeding" the Viewer.

◉ Viewer and Event Viewer

If both Viewers are visible, then it is still important which window pane is selected when hitting the Space Bar. This time however, the video will play either on the Viewer (Project selected) or the Event Viewer (Event selected).

Here is a quick overview of the control elements on the Viewer.

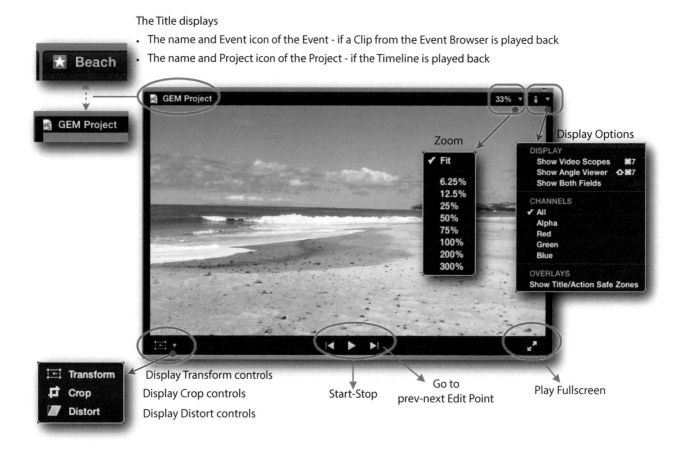

The Title displays
- The name and Event icon of the Event - if a Clip from the Event Browser is played back
- The name and Project icon of the Project - if the Timeline is played back

The Viewer windows can be placed on a second connected screen. You can assign a Key Command for that or use the command from the Main Menu: *Window ➤ Show Viewers on Second Display*

Use the *View ➤ A/V Output* option from the Main Menu to display the Viewer also on a connected Broadcast monitor.

Clips

When we drag an Event Clip from the Event Browser to the Project Timeline, we actually create a NEW Clip.

Remember, I made the distinction earlier that there are three incarnations of a Source Media File:
- **Media File** (in the Finder): The original file (video, audio or still image).
- **Event Clip** (in the Event): The Clip listed in the Event Browser that becomes a (linked) representation of the Media File after it gets imported.
- **Timeline Clip** (on the Timeline): This is the Clip in the Project Timeline that is linked to the Event Clip in the Event.

Clip Appearance

Let's have a closer look at the appearance of a Clip in the Event compared to Clips on the Timeline.
- ☺ Clips with video content (video and still images) are blue and audio only Clips are green.
- ☺ If the Clip carries audio content, then it displays the audio waveform with color coded audio level information from green to yellow to red (audio clipping).
- ☺ In the Event Browser, the Clip is represented by a thumbnail image that functions as a mini-Viewer when using the *"Skimming"* (Key Command *S*). When activated, rolling over the Clip with the mouse will scrub the Clip.
  Toggle audio skimming on/off with the Key Command *sh+S*.

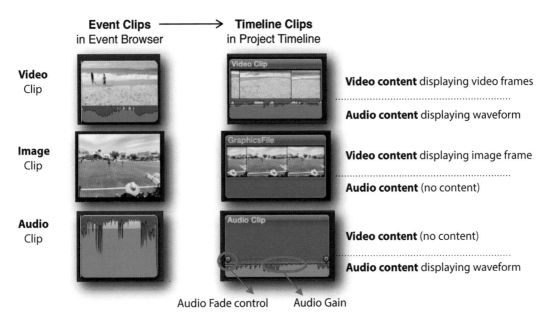

The Timeline Clip has two extra features:
- **Audio Volume**: A Volume line in the audio portion lets you offset the audio level between +12dB and -96 dB by dragging the line up or down. The color-coded waveform will immediately reflect the gain change so you can see if you are clipping the audio (red). This line is also used for volume automation, called *"Audio Animation"*.
- **Audio Fade Handles**: A Clip that has audio content will display two nodes at the clip border when you move the mouse over the audio content. *Dragging* those nodes horizontally will create an audio fade in or audio fade out. The waveform displays a visual representation of the fade curve.

Adjustment pop-up menu: Earlier versions of FCPx displayed a little Adjustment button in the upper left corner of a Timeline Clip. This opened a popup menu for various clip "treatments". That icon is gone and the commands are now available in different locations.

There is a separate *Clip Appearance* window that can be opened by clicking on the switch in the lower right corner of the Timeline window. It provides four display settings for the Timeline Clips:

- **Display Content**: Choose from six clip types with different proportions between audio and video content. Use the Key Command *ctr+opt+ArrowUp* or *ctr+opt+ArrowDown* to step through the six different types or use the dedicated number 1-6 with the modifier key *ctr+opt* to switch to a specific display type.

- **Clip Height**: Adjust the height of the Clips with the slider.

- **Show Connections**: Lets you hide the connection line from Connected Clips.

- **Show:** Choose what to display as the Clip Name: *"Clip Names"*, *"Clip Names or Angles"*, *"Clip Roles"*

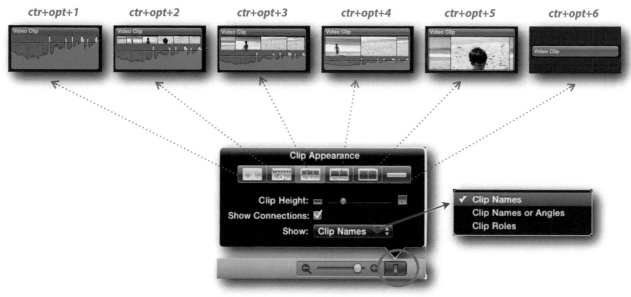

Shortcut Menus

Both, the Event Clips in the Event Browser and the Timeline Clips in the Project Timeline, have individual Shortcut Menus when you *ctr+click* on the Clip.

Most of the commands are advanced features that I will cover in my second Manual *"Final Cut Pro X - The Details"*, but I want to point out a few commands that we have discussed already.

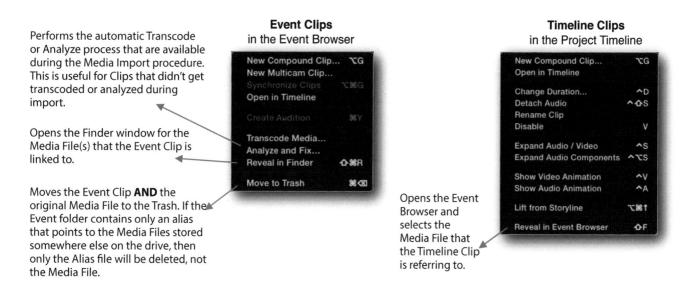

Performs the automatic Transcode or Analyze process that are available during the Media Import procedure. This is useful for Clips that didn't get transcoded or analyzed during import.

Opens the Finder window for the Media File(s) that the Event Clip is linked to.

Moves the Event Clip **AND** the original Media File to the Trash. If the Event folder contains only an alias that points to the Media Files stored somewhere else on the drive, then only the Alias file will be deleted, not the Media File.

Event Clips
in the Event Browser

New Compound Clip... ⌥G
New Multicam Clip...
Synchronize Clips ⌥⌘G
Open in Timeline

Create Audition ⌘Y

Transcode Media...
Analyze and Fix...
Reveal in Finder ⇧⌘R

Move to Trash ⌘⌫

Timeline Clips
in the Project Timeline

New Compound Clip... ⌥G
Open in Timeline

Change Duration... ^D
Detach Audio ^⇧S
Rename Clip
Disable V

Expand Audio / Video ^S
Expand Audio Components ^⌥S

Show Video Animation ^V
Show Audio Animation ^A

Lift from Storyline ⌥⌘↑

Reveal in Event Browser ⇧F

Opens the Event Browser and selects the Media File that the Timeline Clip is referring to.

FCPx has two types of Playheads, the Playhead and the Skimmer. There is a very flexible system behind this that enables you to control the playback of your Project or your Clips based on various conditions. However, with flexibility often comes complexity. So please, read the following section carefully to understand what plays back when and why.

Playhead

This is the a standard component known from other video editors or audio production applications. Some sort of triangle marker on the Time Ruler that extends as a vertical line across the Timeline area. It moves horizontally along the Timeline to indicate at what time position the Project is currently parked at or playing back.

FCPx has two variations of such a Playheads, one on the Project Timeline and one for Event Clips in the Event Browser.

➡ *Playhead on the Timeline*

This is the standard Playhead functionality.

- 🌙 Position the Playhead by moving the "head" along the Time Ruler.
- 🌙 Using any of the playback controls will move the Playhead accordingly.
- 🌙 The Playhead position is displayed in the SMPTE Reader on the Toolbar and the displayed in the Viewer.
- 🌙 The Playhead is read (when Skimming is active, the Playhead turns white in Stop mode).

➡ *Playhead on the Event Clips*

The Event Browser uses a variation of the standard Playhead. It allows the playback of a single Event Clip that is represented by a thumbnail image or a filmstrip (a series of thumbnail images). These thumbnails represent a virtual timeline of that Clip from the left to the right border of the image without any Time Ruler on top.

- 🌙 Click on the thumbnail to position the Playhead which will appear as a white vertical line.
- 🌙 The actual timing position is displayed in the SMPTE Reader on the Toolbar. It is either the relative time from the left to the right border of the Clip or retrieved from the embedded timecode of the Clip.
- 🌙 A little black info window on top of the Playhead will be displayed to show the name of the Clip plus the timing position. It is on when you skim over and stays for a few seconds when you stop the movement. This is called the "Skimmer Info" which can be toggled with the Key Command *ctr+Y* or the Menu Command *View ➤ Show/Hide Skimmer Info* (The Event Browser window has to be selected to use that menu command).

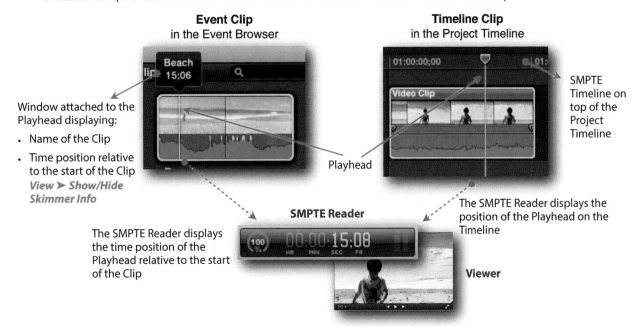

Event Clip in the Event Browser

Timeline Clip in the Project Timeline

Window attached to the Playhead displaying:
- Name of the Clip
- Time position relative to the start of the Clip
View ➤ Show/Hide Skimmer Info

Playhead

SMPTE Timeline on top of the Project Timeline

SMPTE Reader

The SMPTE Reader displays the time position of the Playhead relative to the start of the Clip

The SMPTE Reader displays the position of the Playhead on the Timeline

Viewer

Skimmer

The second type of Playhead is called a *Skimmer* or *Skimming Bar*.

Skimming is like an active scrubbing feature with your mouse cursor similar to an old reel-to-reel tape or video machine where in pause mode, the tape or film is still engaged against the Playhead. When you spin the reels, the audio and video is playing back, responding to the movement. Activating Skimming is like putting FCPx in this "play-pause" mode. Any movement with your mouse will move the Skimmer and therefore plays back the Clip.

- You use the Skimmer to "search through" a Clip (scrubbing) by moving the mouse across the Clip or to place the Skimmer at a specific position in the Clip.
- The Skimmer position is also displayed in the SMPTE Reader on the Toolbar. And the Viewer
- The Skimmer is indicated by a red vertical line.
- Moving the mouse over the Event Clip or the Timeline Clip will also switch key focus between Event and Project.
- Once you hit the *Space* Bar, FCPx starts playing back with the regular Playhead from the current Skimmer position.
- The Skimmer position has also priority over the Playhead when zooming in and out of the Timeline. The zoom centers around the Skimmer.

FCPx has actually two Skimming modes. One is the main *Skimming* mode and the second one is *Clip Skimming*, a special mode that changes the Skimming behavior for Timeline Clips. The implementation of both modes is not really that elegant and can cause some confusion.

➡ *Skimming*

You can toggle the Skimming feature with these three commands:

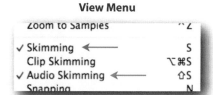

View Menu

- Main Menu *View ➤ Skimming*
- Key Command *S*
- Skimming button  in the upper right corner of the Project window

You can disable the audio portion (mute) during skimming with the following commands

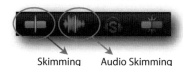

Timeline Buttons

Skimming   Audio Skimming

- Main Menu *View ➤ Audio Skimming*
- Key Command *sh+S*
- Audio Skimming button  in the upper right corner of the Project window

The Skimming feature works the same when scrubbing over Event Clips in the Event Browser or scrubbing along the Project Timeline. Skimming is also available in the Project Library to skim along the filmstrips representing the various Projects. Video skimming is always active regardless of the Skimming setting but Audio skimming has to be activated (*sh+S*) separately.

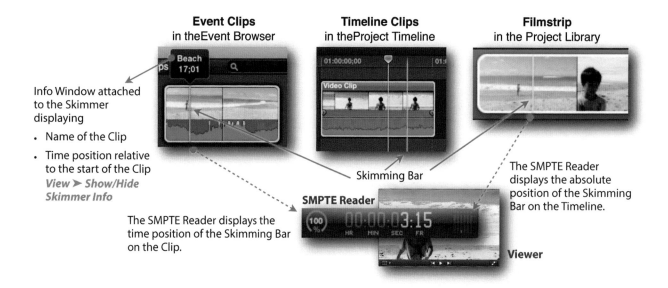

Event Clips
in theEvent Browser

Timeline Clips
in theProject Timeline

Filmstrip
in the Project Library

Info Window attached to the Skimmer displaying
- Name of the Clip
- Time position relative to the start of the Clip
  View ➤ Show/Hide Skimmer Info

Skimming Bar

SMPTE Reader

The SMPTE Reader displays the time position of the Skimming Bar on the Clip.

The SMPTE Reader displays the absolute position of the Skimming Bar on the Timeline.

Viewer

➡ Clip Skimming

Clip Skimming is a special Skimming Mode that affects only the Timeline, not the skimming of Event Clips. It can be activated independently of the regular Skimming function. Please pay attention how it is implemented.

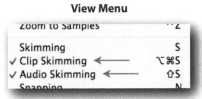

View Menu

You can toggle the Clip Skimming feature with any of these two commands.

- 💡 Menu Command *View ➤ Clip Skimming*
- 💡 Key Command *opt+cmd+S*

You can disable the audio portion (mute) during skimming with the following commands

- 💡 Main Menu *View ➤ Audio Skimming*
- 💡 Key Command *sh+S*

How Clip Skimming works

▶ **Clip Skimming off**: This is the regular behavior. When moving around in the Timeline with the mouse, ALL the Clips are "played" and you can see the red Skimming bar going across all clips ❶. Only the horizontal position (time) is relevant.

▶ **Clip Skimming on**: This adds a "Solo" functionality to the Skimming. When you move over a Clip, only that Clip will be skimmed and all the other Clips that are "present" at that same time location are muted. The red Skimmer bar is now only visible on that Clip ❷. If you move the mouse over an area in the Timeline, not covering any Clip, then the Clip Skimming is ignored and all Clips are played ❸ at that position (but only if the regular Skimming is on).

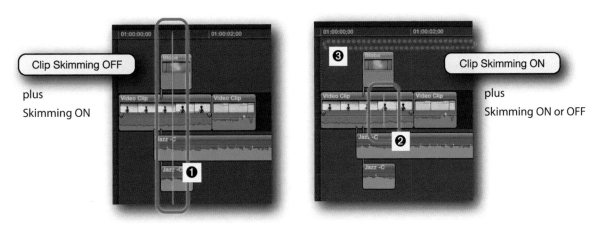

Please note that the two Skimming icons at the upper right corner of the Timeline only belong to the "Skimming" feature and NOT to the "Clip Skimming" feature.

The Skimming icon indicates whether or not "Skimming" is activated. There is no visual feedback if *Clip Skimming* is activated.

The Audio Skimming icon only relates to the Skimming feature, not the Clip Skimming feature. Whether or not audio is activated during Clip Skimming is only determined by its checkmark in the View Menu, even if this icon is disabled.

Skimming Commands - Summary

What looks like three separate Skimming options in the View menu that can be toggled on/off, is in fact a combination of those three options.

- **Skimming**: Plays video of all Clips ❶.
- **Clip Skimming**: Plays video of only the current ("moved over") Clip ❷.
- **Skimmer + Clip Skimming**: Plays video of only the "moved over Clips ❷ or all the Clips when moving outside ❸.
- **Audio Skimming**: This just turns the audio content of the Clip(s) on/off for any combination above. Selecting Audio Skimming alone doesn't do anything.

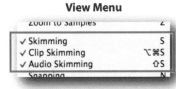

View Menu

Most of the time you don't need the entire Clip when choosing an Event Clip that you want to use in the Timeline. Maybe there is some stuff at the beginning and at the end that isn't useful. Maybe it's a longer Clip that has multiple scenes or takes in it or different sections that you might use at different places in your final sequence. You go ahead and mark those sections as "**Subclips**".

> **A Subclip is a section of an Event Clip**

Creating a Subclip is easy. Select a specific Range in the Event Clip and mark that section as a Subclip, maybe giving it a suitable name so you can easily find (search for) it later. The Subclip is just an *instruction* that says "play the Event Clip X from time position A to time position B".

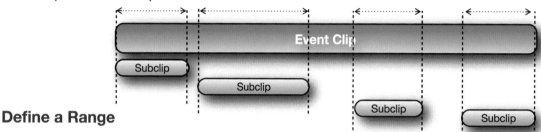

Define a Range

You mark a section of a Clip by defining a Range.

- ☑ Select the Event Clip from the Event Browser.
- ☑ Start playing back the Clip and watch it in the Viewer (or in the Clip itself that acts like a mini-Viewer).
- ☑ When the Clip reaches the position where you want to start your selection, hit the *I* key to mark the IN point.
- ☑ When the Clip reaches the position where you want to end your selection, hit the *O* key to mark the OUT point.

Mark	Clip	Modify	Window	Help
Set Range Start				I
Set Range End				O
Set Clip Range				X
Clear Selected Ranges				⌥X

- ☑ You could also just draw the Range by *click-drag* directly on the Clip (use the Skimming feature for better orientation). Once a Range is displayed with yellow borders, you cannot click drag inside that marked Range anymore.
- ☑ To adjust the Range, *drag* the left or right border of the marked Range.
- ☑ The Clip "remembers" its defined Range when you switch between different Clips in the Event Browser.

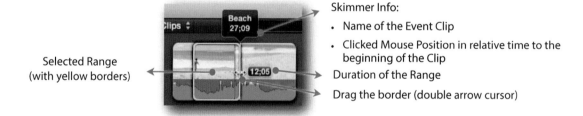

Selected Range
(with yellow borders)

Skimmer Info:
- Name of the Event Clip
- Clicked Mouse Position in relative time to the beginning of the Clip

Duration of the Range

Drag the border (double arrow cursor)

Define Multiple Ranges on a Clip

Dragging a Range on a Clip will remove any previous Range unless you use *cmd+drag*. This lets you define multiple Ranges. Use the Key Commands *sh+cmd+I* and *sh+cmd+O* to add additional Ranges during playback. Now you can assign a Keyword to multiple Ranges at once or drag multiple Ranges to the Timeline at once.

Ranges are now remembered when you switch between Event Clips.

Key Command *X* selects the entire Clip and *opt+X* clears any current Range. This is also available from the *Mark* Menu.

3 Types of Subclips

Now is the first time that we are getting more into Metadata and related concepts. I didn't discuss it in the Event Chapter but I want to point something out here. Many Editors might not like the new concept in FCPx with the Events, Keywords, Ratings, Smart Collections etc. They may not realize that FCPx incorporates a concept known as "Digital Asset Management" (DAM). This is used in huge databases to manage those datasets efficiently. Although mainly used in big corporate systems (banks, manufacturing, etc), it has moved into our smaller systems like iTunes and iPhoto with their Ratings and Smart Playlists. Even the Finder with its Smart Folders and Spotlight uses principles of Digital Asset Management to manage our ever growing data sets, (files, photos, songs, etc). Let me try to compare the old and new FCP with that aspect in mind.

Old FCP concept	New FCPx concept
You are in charge of how to manually organize your Clips. This lets you have the ultimate flexibility since you are in charge of managing the files. However, that "managing" process can become very overwhelming with the increase of files and the final goal of "finding the right Clip - fast" could be jeopardized.	You are in charge of how to describe the Clips (metadata). FCPx then finds your Clips automatically based on those descriptions and search queries. This requires an understanding of "data management" that might be unfamiliar to some people. It also means, "letting go" and trusting the system. You don't go to a particular bin anymore, knowing that you put specific Clips there. Now you go to particular Smart Collections where the system "displays" specific Clips based on your metadata and search queries. If used in the right way the whole system becomes extremely flexible and fast. But it requires a new "mind set" from the Editor.

So let's dive into metadata territory a little bit.

FCPx uses three types of Subclips. Although their concept is the same (marking a sub-section of the Event Clip), they are used differently. The three kinds of Subclips are like three kinds of Metadata, similar to fields in a database. "Markers" are a fourth kind of metadata but they don't describe a Subclip (a Range), just one single address (one position).

- **Analysis**: This type of metadata is created automatically by FCPx. It can analyze the Media File and look for specific characteristics, like if the camera has excessive shake (and therefore the footage might not be of any use). Or it can analyze to see when the footage has close-ups of one, two or three people in the shot. Let's say you have two hours of raw video imported. Now with the click of a button you can go directly to the scenes that have two people in them. No need to preview the two hours manually, making notes and Clips and organizing them in bins (yes, the analyze process is automatic, so your milage may vary regarding the accuracy). If an Event Clip has one of those tags, then FCPx automatically creates a dynamic *Smart Collection* (like an automatic bin) for each individual tag in the Event Library inside that Event.
  Analyzed subclips have a purple gear icon 🟣 in the Event Browser.

- **Keyword**: This is a simple form of a metadata. You create Subclips by assigning them specific tags (a word or phrase). This way you can mark similar scenes (Indoor, Car Ride, Cloudy Day, etc ...) with the same tag. You can see in the Event Browser if an Event Clip has one of those Subclips. FCPx also creates a dynamic *Keyword Collection* (like an automatic bin) for each individual tag in the Event Library for that Event. Now with one click, you can see all the "Indoor" or "Car Ride" subclips together for easy selection.
  Keyword subclips have a blue Key icon 🔑 in the Event Browser.

- **Rating:** This is actually a dual Metatag. You can mark a section as **Favorite** ⭐ or **Rejected** ❌. This way you can later select all your favorite scenes or let FCPx filter out all the sections that are marked "Rejected" (shaky camera, outtakes, etc). It's important to know that you can rename the Ratings subclip and even search for those names.
  You can create a Smart Collection manually in the Event Library to include Ratings tags.

Create Subclips

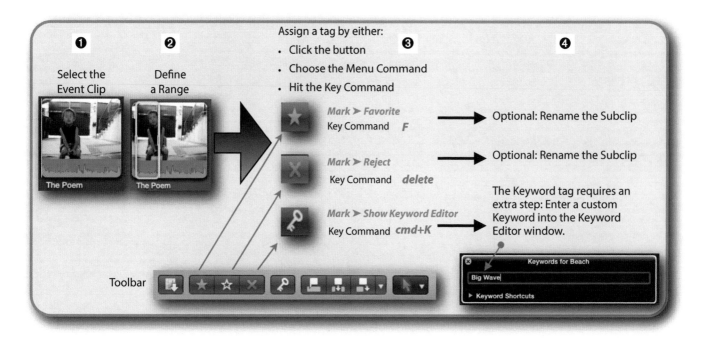

❶ Select the Event Clip

❷ Define a Range

Assign a tag by either:
- Click the button
- Choose the Menu Command
- Hit the Key Command

❸

Mark ➤ Favorite
Key Command **F**

➤ Optional: Rename the Subclip

Mark ➤ Reject
Key Command **delete**

➤ Optional: Rename the Subclip

Mark ➤ Show Keyword Editor
Key Command **cmd+K**

➤ The Keyword tag requires an extra step: Enter a custom Keyword into the Keyword Editor window.

❹

Toolbar

Keywords for Beach
Big Wave
▶ Keyword Shortcuts

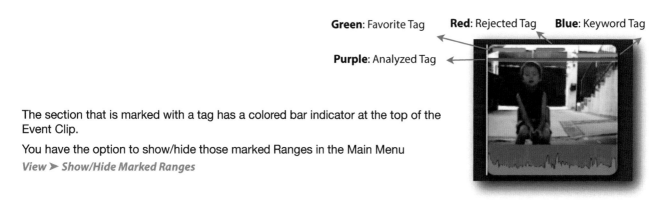

Green: Favorite Tag   **Red**: Rejected Tag   **Blue**: Keyword Tag

Purple: Analyzed Tag

The section that is marked with a tag has a colored bar indicator at the top of the Event Clip.

You have the option to show/hide those marked Ranges in the Main Menu

View ➤ Show/Hide Marked Ranges

All the Subclips are listed in the Event Browser "inside" the Event Clip (with a disclosure triangle like a folder in the Finder).

If you select any of the Subclips, a white border on the thumbnail marks the Range of the Subclip that reflects its length in relation to the whole Event Clip (total width of the thumbnail image).

➡ Keyword Editor

The Key button on the Toolbar is actually a toggle button for the Keyword Editor window "open-close". If it is gray, then the Keyword window isn't open. If you click on it, then the button turns blue indicating that the Keyword Editor is now open.

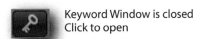 Keyword Window is closed
Click to open

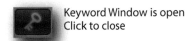 Keyword Window is open
Click to close

➡ Keyword Shortcuts

The Keyword Editor (a floating window) has a disclosure triangle that reveals the *Keyword Shortcuts.*

You can pre-assign Keywords to the available nine Key Commands. Next time you want to assign a Keyword to a Subclip, just select the Range in the Event Clip and hit the assigned Key Command to assign that Keyword to that Subclip. No need to open the Keyword Editor and type in the actual Keyword.

Keyword Editor

➡ Removing/Converting Tags

Remove Analysis Tag

Ctr+click on an Analysis Subclip to open its Shortcut Menu and select *"Remove Analysis Keywords"*.

You can also use the other commands to quickly re-assign a Favorite or Reject tag to that Subclip.

Remove Ratings Tag

Ctr+click on a Favorite or Reject Subclip to open its Shortcut Menu and select *"Unmark"*.

You can also change the Subclip from Favorite to Reject and vice versa or click on the opposite Star button in the Toolbar.

The grey Star button on the Toolbar works as an *"Unmark"* button.

Remove Keyword Tag

Ctr+click on the Keyword Subclip in the Event Browser to open its Shortcut Menu and select *"Remove all Keywords"*. All Keywords is referring to the Keywords in that particular Subclip not all the Keywords in the entire Event Clip.

You can also convert the Subclip into a Favorite or Reject tag by selecting the command from the Menu.

If you use the Main Menu Command *Mark ➤ Remove All Keywords*, then you can select either the entire Clip in the Browser (to delete all Keywords in that Clip) or just its Keyword selection (to delete that Keywords in that section).

Selecting a Keyword Selection in the Event Browser displays that Keyword in the Keyword Editor window (if it's visible). Now you can delete individual Keywords if a selection has more than one Keyword. Select it and press *delete.*

The Keyword Collection in the Event Library will not be deleted when you delete the actual Keyword from a Clip. That Collection can only be deleted manually with the Shortcut Menu

As I mentioned in the previous section, a Marker can be considered a "special type of Subclip". Instead of defining an in and out position, Markers define only one position, one timecode address.

So instead of Ranges, they are reference points for all kinds of purposes. For example, mark a specific spot (and add notes and instructions to it) that you can easily find later, mark spots for synchronizations (door slams) or use it to create chapters that are carried over to your exported file (QuickTIme, Podcast, DVD, etc).

FCPx provides four types of Markers:

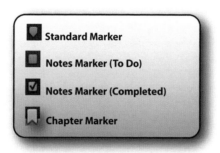

Where can I use Markers

Before learning how to assign and manage Markers, let's get an overview of where and when those Markers are used and displayed.

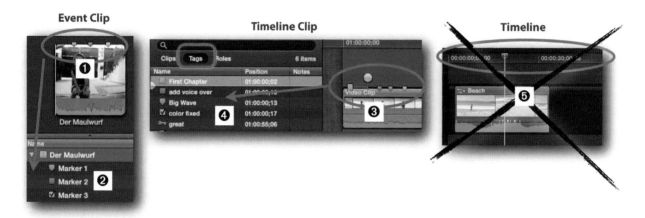

🌀 **Event**

    ❶ **Event Clip**: Markers can be attached to Event Clips in the Event Browser. They will be visible on top of the Clip.

    ❷ **Event Bower** (List View): The Markers assigned to an Event Clip are visible in the Browser's List View "inside" the Clip as separate entries together with other Metadata for that Clip.

🌀 **Project**

    ❸ **Timeline Clip**: Markers can be attached to Timeline Clips. They will be visible on top of the Clip. When an Event Clip gets moved to the Timeline, it brings its Markers with it and you can create more on the Timeline Clip.

    ❹ **Timeline Index**: Markers on Timeline Clips are also listed in the Timeline Index under the "*Tags*" tab. This lists all the Markers of all the Clips on the Timeline together with all other Metadata assigned to any Clip on the Timeline.

🌀 **Timeline**

    ❺ Markers CANNOT be assigned directly to the Timeline, they have to belong to a Clip.
Tip: Create a Placeholder Clip as a Connected Clip on the first frame of the Primary Storyline and extend it to the end of the Project Timeline. Now you can create Markers on that long "Pseudo Timeline Clip".

        6 - Clips

Create and Manage Clips

A variety of commands lets you manage Markers through Key Commands, Main Menus and Shortcut Menus:

▶ **Create** a Marker: Click *M* to create a Marker (on the Event Clip in the Event Browser or on a Timeline Clip in the Timeline) at the current Playhead/Skimmer position in Stop or Play mode. This creates a blue Standard Marker .

▶ Create Marker and Modify: *Opt+M* creates a Marker, stops playback and opens the *Marker Window*.

▶ **Modify** a Marker: *Click* on the Marker, either on the Clip or in the List. This will move the Playhead to that position. Now click again or press *M* again to open the *Marker Window*.

▶ **Delete** a Marker: A single Marker or all the markers in a selection. Use the available commands or click the delete button in the Marker Window.

▶ **Nudge** a Marker: You can nudge the Markers left or right by 1 frame (or 1 subframe for audio only Clips). Key Command *ctr+,* or *ctr+.*

▶ **Next - Previous** Marker: Use the Key Command *ctr+;* and *ctrl+'* or the Menu Command *Mark ➤ Previous ➤ Marker* and *Mark ➤ Next ➤ Marker*

▶ **Copy-Paste**: Use the *Cut Marker* or *Copy Marker* command from the Shortcut Menu and paste the Marker at the Playhead position with the Key Command *cmd+V*.

Marker Window

Here is a table with all the four Marker types, what their icons look like and what is displayed in the Marker Window when you open it from a specific marker. The window is context sensitive, which means, depending on what kind of Marker you selected, it will only display options that make sense in that context.

● **Marker Type**: These tabs on top of the window let you choose (change) the Marker Type. Please note that Chapter Markers are not available for Event Clips, only for Timeline Clips.

● **Name**: Enter a name or description for the Marker in the entry box. That name can also be changed in the Timeline Index.

● **To Do - Complete**: For Notes Marker, an additional checkbox (*Completed*) lets you switch the status between "To Do" and "Completed".

● **Position**: The SMPTE location of the marker is just a display. You have to use the Nudge command if you want to move an existing Marker.

● **Delete**: Click this button to delete this Marker.

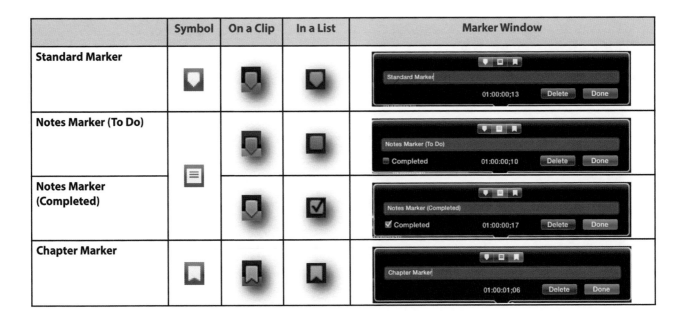

	Symbol	On a Clip	In a List	Marker Window
Standard Marker				Standard Marker — 01:00:00;13 — Delete — Done
Notes Marker (To Do)				Notes Marker (To Do) — ☐ Completed — 01:00:00;10 — Delete — Done
Notes Marker (Completed)				Notes Marker (Completed) — ☑ Completed — 01:00:00;17 — Delete — Done
Chapter Marker				Chapter Marker — 01:00:01;06 — Delete — Done

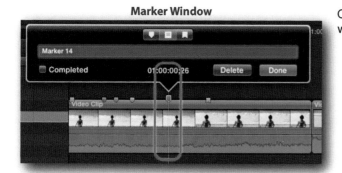

Opening the Marker Window for any Marker will position that window just above the Clip, centered at that selected Marker.

➡ *Timeline Index*

The two icons for the Notes Marker in the Timeline Index are actually active checkboxes. Click on it to check or uncheck that icon and therefore toggle its status between "To Do" and Completed".

At the bottom of the Timeline Index are buttons that lets you filter the List to display only a specific type of Marker (or Keywords and Analysis tags).

Timeline Index

Click to
• check
• uncheck

Filter

Chapter Markers

A Chapter Marker is a special type of Marker.

- Chapter Markers can only be created on Timeline Clips.

- Chapter Markers can be exported together with the video when checked in the Share Settings. Those Chapter Markers are supported by a wide variety of applications (Quicktime, iTunes DVD Player) and devices (iDevices, DVD players). They are embedded as metadata in mp4, m4v and mov export formats. Use them as chapters in a quicktime movie, chapters for podcasts and even chapters used in Compressor for encoding purposes. Chapter Markers can also be used for subtitles when exporting a project to DVD or Blue-ray.

- When selecting a Chapter Marker on the Timeline Clip, an attached Poster Frame pin will be displayed. You can drag that orange pin left or right to position it on a frame. This becomes the Poster Frame that is displayed later as the Marker reference in the QuickTime movie.

Export to Quicktime: Share Settings

Export to DVD: Share Settings

➡ *Chapter Marker Thumbnail*

Each Chapter Marker will include a still image, the so called Chapter Marker Thumbnail or Poster Frame. This image will be used as a visual representation of the Marker.

When selecting a Chapter Marker on a Timeline Clip, a Pin will be displayed with the Chapter Marker. This Pin marks the position of the frame that is used as the thumbnail. The default position is 11 frames next to the Marker but you can drag the pin left and right to choose the right frame. The Viewer will display the frame of the pin position when dragging. You can drag the pin anywhere from the beginning to the end of the Primary Storyline. If the Marker is on a Connected Storyline, then you can move the pin between the beginning and end of that storyline.

Chapter Marker Thumbnail
Chapter Marker

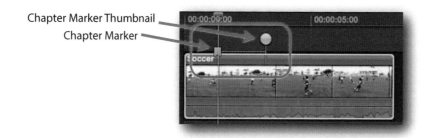

Placing a Clip

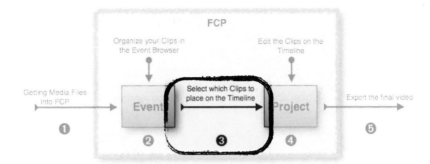

Now that we've organized all our source material as Event Clips in the Event, we can finally go to the next level and place the Clips onto the Timeline to create our video. In order to do that, we have to ask ourselves four fundamental questions:

?	What	**What** Clip(s) from the Event Browser do we want to place onto the Timeline?
🔧	How	**How** do we move the Clip, with what command or action?
→	Where	**Where** on the Timeline do we want the Clip to be placed?
⚡	Consequences	What are the **Consequences** to the existing Clips on the Timeline?

What **Clip to Select**

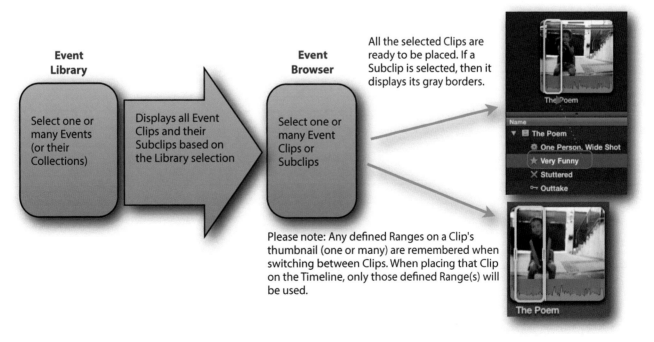

How to place the Clip

Content Filter

Whatever method you choose to place a Clip from the Event Browser to the Project Timeline, there is an important filter that you have to be aware of. Whenever you do that action, you can choose:

- **Use All**: The entire Clip, Video and Audio.
- **Use Video Only**: Only the Video portion of the Clip.
- **Use Audio Only**: Only the Audio portion of the Clip.

> Keep in mind that you always move a Clip (or Subclip) not its individual content, you just decide what is "in it". Overwriting a video+audio clip with an audio only clip doesn't just replace the audio portion, it replaces the original video and audio portion, in that case with no video.

Whatever method you are using to place a Clip on the Timeline, that command is always executed with the currently set filter. You can change the filter in three different ways (This filter doesn't apply when dragging Clips from the Media Browser or the Finder!)

- Use a Key Command: All *sh+1*, Video Only *sh+2*, Audio Only *sh+3*
- Select a Menu Command *Edit ➤ Source Media ➤*
- Click on the "Triangle" in the Toolbar to select from that popup menu

Pay attention to the details:

The buttons actually change their appearance depending on the current filter setting. This conforms with the basic FCPx color code for the Clips: video=blue and audio=green

2 ways to move:

There are basically two methods to move Event Clip(s) or Subclip(s) from the Event Browser onto the Project Timeline:

- **Commands**: You can choose from a variety of commands to move the selected Event Clip from the Event Browser directly onto the Timeline in the Project.
- **Drag-and-Drop**: You can use your mouse to drag a Clip from the Event Browser directly onto the Timeline in the Project.

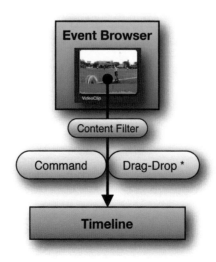

* Remember that you can also drag files from the Media Browser or directly from the Finder onto the Timeline (they get automatically added to the Default Event)

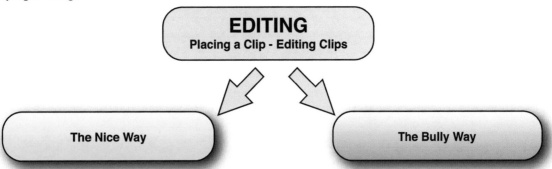

EDITING
Placing a Clip - Editing Clips

The Nice Way

Clips get adjusted to new situations and moved around to find "compromises"

This is the **default** behavior in FCPx when placing Clips or editing Clips on the Timeline. Existing Clips on the Timeline will automatically move out of the way when inserting new Clips. Or when moving a Clip out of a sequence or deleting it, the gap will close up, moving the rest of the Clips to the left, always guaranteeing that the Clips on the Timeline stay connected. It is the new *"Magnetic Timeline"*.

The Bully Way

Clips get deleted and overwritten when they are in the way and "special gaps" are left behind

This is the **exception** in FCPx when placing Clips or editing Clips on the Timeline. This time, placing a Clip on the Timeline will OVERWRITE whatever Clip is there and when moving a Clip, the rest of the Timeline Clips will not try to close the empty space, instead FCPx will leave a "Gap Clip" behind. On a side note: Nothing gets shifted on the Timeline, which might sometimes be exactly what you want.

➡ *Use a Command*

So how many different commands are there for placing a Clip onto the Timeline? It depends on how you count:

- 💡 There are four main methods: **Connect - Insert - Append - Overwrite**
- 💡 Three of those methods have a "variation": **Backtimed Connect - Backtimed Insert - Backtimed Overwrite**

- 💡 On top of that, there are three ways to initiate the command:
  - ▶ Select a Menu Command
  - ▶ Click on a button in the Toolbar
  - ▶ Use a Key Command

    (Remember, whatever method you are using, that command is always executed with the currently set content filter)

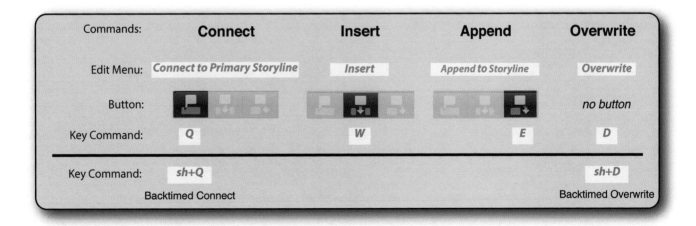

Commands:	**Connect**	**Insert**	**Append**	**Overwrite**
Edit Menu:	*Connect to Primary Storyline*	*Insert*	*Append to Storyline*	*Overwrite*
Button:				*no button*
Key Command:	Q	W	E	D
Key Command:	sh+Q			sh+D
	Backtimed Connect			Backtimed Overwrite

The "Overwrite" command follows the "bully way". Maybe that's why it didn't get its own button and is only available as a command.

➡ *Use Drag-and-Drop*

Instead of selecting the Event Clip(s) in the Event Browser and initiating one of the commands, you can use the mouse and just drag them down to the Project Timeline. You can make the choice by dragging exactly the item you want:

❶ Select one or many Clips in the Event Browser and *drag* them to the Timeline. If more than one Clip was selected, then dragging one Clip will move all the selected Clips with them. You will actually see the names of the Clips while you are dragging the cursor.

❷ If the selection is displayed as a white border on the Event Browser filmstrip, then you can drag inside that border to move it down to the Timeline (the border will change to a yellow Range selection).

❸ You can also define ad-hoc Range(s) and drag those sections of the Clip down to the Project Timeline.

Event Browser

Drag item from the list

Event Browser

Drag Subclip selection in filmstrip

Event Browser

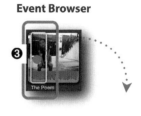

Drag Range(s)

▶ **Use Drag-and-Drop** (not from the Event Browser)

The proper way in FCPx is to import the Media Files first into Events and then drag those Event Clips from the Event Browser to the Project Timeline. But there are two exceptions as we have seen in the Import chapter:

- Drag Media Files to the Timeline from the Media Browser.
- Drag Media Files to the Timeline from the Finder.

Remember, those files get automatically added to the Project's Default Event in the background and you are "invisibly" moving them from the Event Browser following perfect FCPx protocol.

The Import settings in the Preferences window apply to those files (Organize, Transcode, Analyze).

Where to place the Clip

Now we have all those different options on "how" to move the Clip to the Timeline, the next question is, "where" exactly on the Timeline will the Clip be positioned.

➡ *Using Commands*

There are two possible target positions on the Project Timeline to place the new Clip: Playhead/Skimmer or a Range (3-point Edit).

Playhead (or Skimmer)

Selected Range

Define Range:
Key Command *I* and *O* at the Playhead position or use the Range Tool (*R*)

The Clip from the Event Browser will be placed at the Playhead. If a Skimmer Bar is visible then its position has priority.

Only as much of the Clip(s) from the Event Browser will be used to fill up the selected Range in the Timeline. The selected Range can even span across more than one selected Clip on the Timeline.

The example below illustrates the different placement of the Clip when using the regular command (connect, insert, overwrite) or the backtimed variation of those commands:

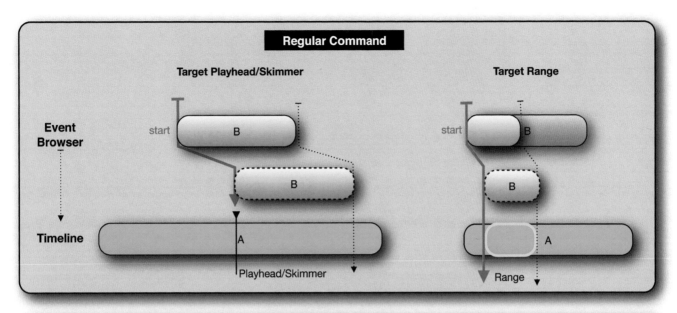

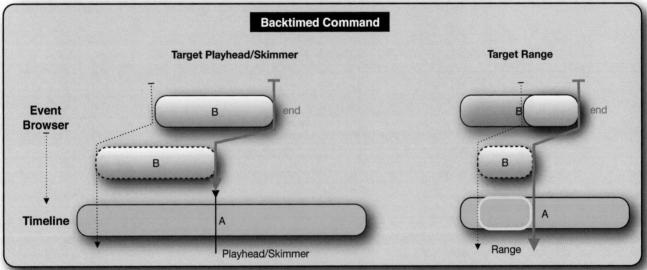

There is an exception for the Playhead position:

▶ The Playhead position will be ignored if you choose the Append command. The new Clip will append to the last Clip on the Timeline (Primary Storyline) regardless of the Playhead position.

➡ *Using Drag-and-Drop*

If you choose Drag-and-Drop to move the Clip from the Event Browser to the Project Timeline, then your mouse position determines where the target position will be on the Timeline. (Playhead/Skimmer or any existing Range selection will be ignored).

Consequences

We've seen many different ways to move Clips from the Event Browser and place them on the Project Timeline. Now, let's explore the different "Consequences" on the Timeline. You have to be aware of what happens to the existing Clips on the Timeline and how they "react" to the "intruder".

And again, those consequences are different if you are using commands or drag-and-drop.

➡ *Using Commands*

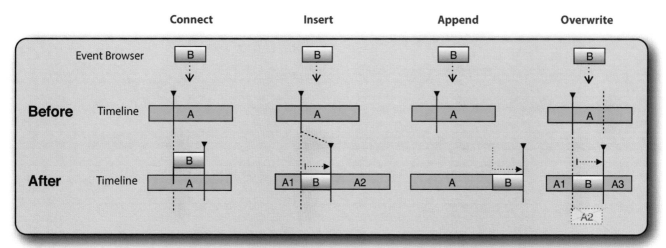

The new Clip (B) gets connected to the Primary Storyline at the Playhead position. The Playhead moves to the end of the new Clip (this is actually a Preference settings *"Position Playhead after Edit Operation"*)

The original Clip (A) gets cut at the Playhead position and the new Clip (B) gets inserted, moving the rest of the Clip A to the right. Everything else after that gets moved to the right too.

The new Clip (B) gets added to the end of the LAST Clip in the Primary Storyline. The original Playhead position is ignored.

The new Clip (B) overwrites the existing Clip at the Playhead position. If Clip B is longer than Clip A, then it continues to overwrite into the next Clip on the Timeline too.

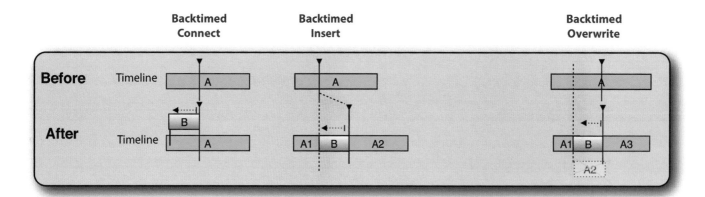

If the Playhead is located later than the end of the last Clip on the Timeline, then FCPx inserts a "Gap Clip" first before adding the new Clip (except for the Append command).

Using Still Images

When putting a still image onto the Timeline which technically has no duration, it will create a Timeline Clip with the length that is set in the Preferences window.

Preferences ➤ Editing

➡ *Using Drag-and-Drop*

There are again two different kinds of consequences when using drag-and-drop with the mouse, depending on what Tool is selected for the cursor when you drag the Clip from the Event Browser down to the Project Timeline. Click on the Tool Selector button in the Toolbar to open the Tools popup menu.

Tools Menu

☠ If the **Position** Tool is selected

Basically, this is the easiest one. Wherever you drop the Clip on the Timeline, that is exactly where it will be. If there is anything in the way, it will be overwritten.

- ▶ If you drop the Clip after the last Clip on the Timeline, then FCPx will create a "Gap Clip" to fill the space.
- ▶ If you drop the Clip on top of an existing Clip, then that Clip will be overwritten for the duration of the new Clip (**Overwrite** functionality).
- ▶ If you drop the Clip above or below the Primary Storyline, then the new Clip will become a Connected Clip (**Connect** functionality).

☺ If the **Select** Tool is selected (or any other Tool besides the Position Tool)

Now Clips are moving out of the way to make room or closing up to fix any possible gap (Magnetic Timeline).

- ▶ If you drop the new Clip after the last existing Clip on the Timeline, then the new Clip will be appended to the end of the last Clip. It is not possible to create a gap, on purpose or by accident (**Append** functionality).
- ▶ If you place the Clip between two adjacent Clips on the Timeline, then the right Clip (and all the rest of the Clips in the Project Timeline) will move to the right to make space for the new Clip. Everything snaps into place to make sure that there are no gaps (**Insert** functionality).
- ▶ It is not possible to split an existing Clip with drag-and-drop. For that you have to use the Insert command with the Playhead.
- ▶ If you place the Clip on top of an existing Clip, then that Clip will fade to gray and a popup menu will open with three options:

  ☺ **Replace**
  Replaces the existing Clip with the new Clip. The rest of the sequence will be shifted to adjust the new length, longer or shorter.

  ☺ **Replace from Start**
  - • If the new Clip is longer than the existing Clip:
    Replaces the existing Clip with footage from the new Clip starting at the first frame for the length of the existing Clip to make sure that the length of the sequence doesn't change.
    If the new Clip is shorter than the existing Clip:
    An Alert Window will pop up to remind you that the new Clip isn't long enough and therefore the sequence will be shortened after the replacement.

  ☺ **Replace from End**
  - • If the new Clip is longer than the existing Clip:
    Replaces the existing Clip with footage from the new Clip starting at the last frame for as long as the length of the existing Clip to make sure that the length of the sequence doesn't change.
  - • If the new Clip is shorter than the existing Clip:
    An Alert Window will pop up to remind you that the new Clip isn't long enough and therefore the sequence will be shortened after the replacement.

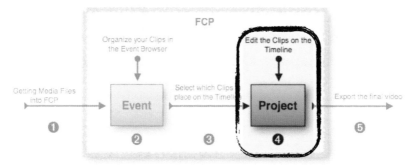

Basics

Once most of the Clips are placed from the Event Browser to the Project Timeline, the next step begins - trimming the Timeline Clips. Of course, new Clips can be added to the Timeline from the Event Browser (or directly from the Finder) at any time during the editing.

Stay in Touch

The Nice Way

The default Clip behavior on the Timeline is that adjacent Clips on the Primary Storyline stay always attached to each other without leaving a gap. Any change you make on the Primary Storyline that affects the length of the existing Clip (lengthen, shortening, inserting, removing) will automatically compensated by FCPx by nicely moving other stuff around. Sometimes you specifically need to leave a gap between Clips. For this purpose there are two kinds of Timeline-special "fake" Clips:

Preferences ➤ Playback

- **Gap**: This is just a black Clip on the Timeline. FCPx creates those Gap Clips automatically (under some circumstances) or you can create a Gap Clip manually with the Menu Command *Edit ➤ Insert Generator ➤ Gap* or the

  Key Command *opt+W.* The Viewer displays a black background or any other of the choices from the *Preferences ➤ Playback* settings.

- **Placeholder**: A Placeholder Clip is similar to a Gap Clip but more sophisticated. You can assign it some properties (in the Inspector) to indicate what it is holding the place for (wide shot, close up, day, night etc). Create a Placeholder Clip with the menu command *Edit ➤ Insert Generator ➤ Placeholder* or Key Command *opt+cmd+W.*

Gap Clips and Placeholder Clips can be named and have Metadata. They show up in the Timeline Index list like any other "regular" Clips.

Gap Clip   **Placeholder Clip**

Editing Tools:

This is the list of available mouse pointers. Use their Key Command or open the popup menu on the Toolbar and select the tool. There is also a nice "temporary tool" feature: Instead of switching the tools back and forth, you can *hold* the Key

Command temporarily while doing the task (cutting, trimming, selecting) and when you're done, let the key go and it will return to the Tool it had before.

- ▶ **Pointer**: Default - all-purpose tool, including ripple trimming.
- ▶ **Trim**: For most of the trimming needs.

The Bully Way

- ▶ **Position**: Move or trim Clips without affecting the Timeline. Overwriting Clips and leaving gaps behind.
- ▶ **Range Selection**: Select a Clip Range (even across multiple Clips).
- ▶ **Blade**: Like a scissor tool to split Clips.
- ▶ **Zoom**: Zoom in (*drag*) and out (*opt+drag*) of the Timeline. Also use *click* and *opt+click.*
- ▶ **Hand**: *Drag* the Timeline (functions like the scroll bar).

🕱 Snapping

Snap Mode snaps objects, borders or Playheads to important positions (start, end of objects, Playhead, Markers) when moving/dragging across the Timeline.

Toggle it on/off with any of the three commands: Snap button in the upper right corner of the Project Timeline, Menu Command *View ➤ Snapping* or Key Command *N* (can be temporarily toggled by holding down the *N* key).

🕱 Fine Trimming

Using *cmd+drag* during any trimming or moving activity with the mouse will switch to a finer moving resolution.

A black info window on top of the Edit Point displays the Timeline position of the Edit Point and the timing offset of your movement. Whatever Time Display setting is selected in the Preferences, applies also to this little info window.

Preferences ➤ Editing ➤ Time Display

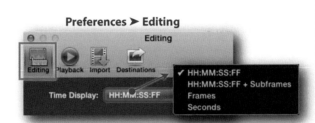

🕱 Split Screen Editing

Enable "*Show detailed trimming feedback*" in the *Preferences ➤ Editing* window to display a two-up Display in the Viewer when performing a trim with the mouse. Now the left display shows the last frame of the left Clip and the right display shows the first frame of the right Clip at the Edit Point. You can temporarily turn it on by holding down the *opt* key while trimming.

Using the *opt* key when the feature is activated, switches the Viewer from displaying the "last Frame left Clip" to the "first Frame right Clip".

Last Frame of left Clip   First Frame of right Clip

🕱 Selections

Please note the difference between a Clip Selection (the whole Clip) and a Range Selection (any portion of it).

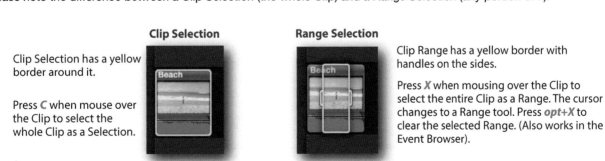

Clip Selection

Clip Selection has a yellow border around it.

Press **C** when mouse over the Clip to select the whole Clip as a Selection.

Range Selection

Clip Range has a yellow border with handles on the sides.

Press **X** when mousing over the Clip to select the entire Clip as a Range. The cursor changes to a Range tool. Press **opt+X** to clear the selected Range. (Also works in the Event Browser).

🌑 Trimming techniques with Edit Points

There are a few trimming techniques that most of the video editing applications use. Those are the ones based on what part of a Clip will be trimmed and what the effect is on the adjacent Clips.

The yellow brackets represent the Edit Point. That's the to-be-edited part of the Clip(s).

| Ripple Left | Ripple Right | Roll | Slip | Slide |

- ▶ **Ripple**: You shorten or lengthen one end of the Clip (left or right) while the adjacent Clip(s) stay "attached" meaning that they get moved to the left or the right on the Timeline to compensate the time difference. (except with the Position Tool). Other Clips on the Timeline will shift.

- ▶ **Roll**: You move two adjacent borders of two Clips together. So one Clip gets shortened while the other one gets lengthened or vice versa. Surrounding Clips will not be affected. Other Timeline Clips stay untouched.

- ▶ **Slip**: You are not moving the Clip. The length of the Clip stays the same and the surrounding Clips and the rest of the Timeline stays untouched. You are only moving the "portion of the media" underneath the Clip, if there is footage available on both ends.

- ▶ **Slide**: This time, the Clip in itself stays untouched (same in, out, length) but you move it, as it is, to the left or the right on the Timeline. Therefore the edges of the Clips to the left and to the right are shortened or lengthened. The rest of the Timeline stays untouched.

🌑 End of Range:

The yellow Edit Point turns to a red border to indicate that there is no more footage at that end of the Clip.

Potential danger with Connected Clips

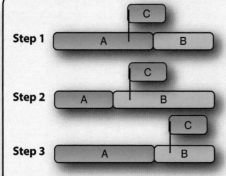

- You have Clip A followed by Clip B. Clip A has a connected Clip C that stays in sync wherever you move Clip A.

- When you shorten Clip A, Clip B will follow (Ripple or Roll). However the Connected Clip C has the "rug pulled out from under it," because this time, it stays in sync with the Timeline and finds a new "mate", Clip B, which it happily attaches to.

- Now, if you extend Clip A, Clip B will be pushed to the right. But this time, the Connected Clip C decides to stick with Clip B and moves with it!

If you did those three steps just to try an edit and you didn't pay attention, then you would have moved Clip C out of its original position. If Clip C was a SFX or a cued music track, then … you are in potential trouble.

Trimming the Clips

What are the different trimming techniques? There are so many different ways to do similar techniques that it can be a bit overwhelming. Here are just a few:

- ▶ **Mouse**: Just slide around the edges of the Clip that you want to trim with the mouse and the correct pointer tool.
- ▶ **SMPTE**: Enter a precise time value of how much you want to trim.
- ▶ **Nudging**: Use Key Commands with predefined time values.
- ▶ **Playhead/Range/Duration**: Use the Playhead or a selected Range for the trim position, or enter a Clip duration.
- ▶ **Split**: Cut up an existing Clip at a specific edit point.

So in all, how many methods are available, and which one is the best to use? More importantly, do they have different effects or limitations?

Let's divide all these trimming techniques into two groups. Editing with commands and editing with the mouse.

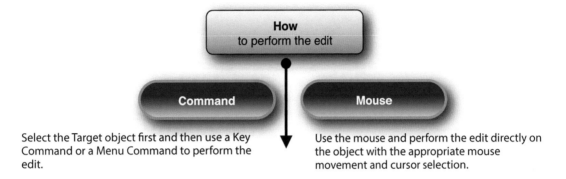

➡ *Using Commands*

When using a command (Key Command or Menu Command), you have to be aware of what the target object will be for your command. That depends mainly on what is selected. It sounds trivial but being aware of who is affected by the command you are using is very crucial because the same command can have different effects depending on what is selected:

- 🔘 **Nothing** is selected
- 🔘 **Clip** is selected
- 🔘 **Range** is selected
- 🔘 **Edit Point** is selected

🔘 Nothing is selected

In this scenario, only the position of the Playhead or Skimmer determines the actual trimming.

- ▶ **Trim Start**: The topmost video clip in the Timeline at the Playhead/Skimmer gets its left edge trimmed to the Playhead/Skimmer position. Any gap will be closed.
  Key Command *opt+[* or Menu Command *Edit ➤ Trim Start*.

- ▶ **Trim End**: The topmost video clip in the Timeline at the Playhead/Skimmer gets its right edge trimmed to the Playhead/Skimmer position. Any gap will be closed.
  Key Command *opt+]* or Menu Command *Edit ➤ Trim End*.

- ▶ **Blade**: The Clip on the Primary Storyline at the Playhead/Skimmer gets cut at the Playhead/Skimmer position, creating two Clips. No change in the Timeline. Key Command *cmd+B* or Menu Command *Edit ➤ Blade*.

  Key Command *sh+cmd+B* or Menu Command *Edit ➤ Blade ALL*. Will split all Clips at the Playhead/Skimmer position.

A Clip is Selected

In this scenario only the selected Clip will be affected:

▶ **Duration**: Changing the duration of a Clip is the same as trimming the end of a Clip. There are four ways to initiate that command. *Double-click* on the SMPTE Reader to enter the duration as an absolute time value. Any of the other three commands will prompt the same SMPTE display: Shortcut Menu command when *ctr+click* on the Clip, use the Key Command *ctr+D* or the Menu Command *Modify ➤ Change Duration...*

▶ **Move by Nudge value:** This moves the selected Clip(s) left or right by the nudge value amount (connected Clips will move in sync). Be careful because this is the "bully way" of editing: Every Clip in the way will be overwritten and potential Gap Clips are left behind. Connected Clips in the way will be "taken over"!

The Bully Way

- Nudge 1 frame left or right with **,** and **.** (the keys with the < and > character)
- Nudge 10 frames left or right with the Key Command *sh+,* (shift and the comma key) and *sh+.*
- Nudge 1 subframe (1/80 frame) left or right with *opt+,* (option and the comma key) and *opt+.*

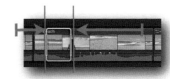

▶ **Move by numerical value:** When a Clip is selected and you hit the + or - Key, the SMPTE Reader changes to a numeric value input device.

The Bully Way

Although the little graphic looks like a "Slide" symbol, this command is NOT a Slide Edit. It is again the "bully way" of editing: Every Clip in the way will be overwritten and potential Gap Clips are left behind.

▶ **Delete:** The selected Clip(s) and its connected Clips will be deleted and any gap will be closed up by the surrounded Clips. Be careful, deleting a Clip on the Primary Storyline will also delete all its Connected Clips. Holding down the "Tilde" key (the ~ in the upper left corner of the keyboard) while hitting the Delete key will keep any Connected Clips.

A Range is Selected

In this scenario the Range selection is used as a guide to trim like there would be one Playhead for the start trim and one for the end trim.

▶ **Trim To Selection**: Use the Menu Command *Edit ➤ Trim to Selection* or the Key Command *opt+* (you can also use the + and - Key to change the duration of the Range). Connected Clips will be affected.

Edit Points are Selected

In this scenario you select the specific Edit Point with the Trim Tool first and then type in the SMPTE Reader the time amount that you want to shift the Edit Point.

This method is for more precise trimming.

☑ You click on the area with the trimming tool to get the yellow border (indicating what trimming technique will be performed on what Clip).

☑ Enter the amount you want to trim in numeric numbers on the keyboard. The numbers, including a graphical indication of the trimming mode, will be displayed in the SMPTE Reader.

Ripple Left

Ripple Right

Roll

Slip

Slide

Move *

Click + or - if you want to move to the left or right, followed by the number entry. Start from right (frames) to left. "23" means "23 frames", "213" means "2sec 13frames". Use the decimal point as a value divider "1." means "1sec 00frames". Use *esc* to abort the process. The number entry has some sort of intelligence: If you work in a 30f format and you type in "35", the display will automatically display "1s 5frames.

* Remember, if a Clip is selected instead of the Edit Point, then the SMPTE displays the Slide symbol when pressing + or -, but it is actually performing a "Position Move".

☑ **Extend Edit** is an additional command that moves the selected Edit Point (the yellow bracket) to the current Playhead/Skimmer position. Use the Menu Command *Edit ➤ Extend Edit* or the Key Command *sh+X.*

➡ *Using the Mouse*

The trimming with commands allows very accurate editing but it requires a two step process of selecting the target first and then applying the command. Trimming with the mouse on the other hand is a more direct and intuitive method because you are performing your edit right there at your finger tips. The mouse cursor in FCPx is now much more flexible, changing its function (and appearance) depending on where you move the mouse over (*location aware*). It requires much less switching of the Pointer Tools. You can even temporarily switch to a different Pointer Tool by holding down the same key that you would normally use to permanently change to that Pointer, perform the action and then release the key. The important thing however is that you always have to be aware of what the current selected Pointer Tool is.

◉ Edit Points

▶ Trim Tool (Select Tool)

Although the Trim Tool provides all the trimming functionality, the default Select Tool provides basic Ripple trimming without the need to switch the cursor to the Trim Tool:

- **Ripple:** *Click* close to the border of a Clip with the Trim Tool *T*. Ripple will also work with the basic Select Tool *A*, so no need to actually switch tools for that.
- **Roll:** *Click* between two adjacent Clips with the Trim Tool *T*.
- **Slip:** *Drag* the Region left or right with the Trim Tool *T*.
- **Slide:** *Opt+drag* the Region left or right with the Trim Tool *T*.

The mouse cursor automatically changes to a different icon when moved over specific areas of the Clip to indicate the current trimming mode.

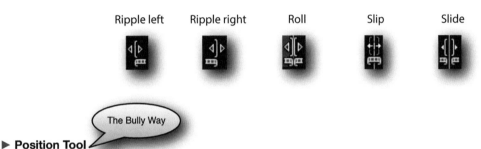

| Ripple left | Ripple right | Roll | Slip | Slide |

▶ Position Tool

The Bully Way

This is the editing mode where FCPx does not try to fill any gaps or move Clips out of the way to make room for an inserted or extended Clip ("Magnetic Timeline function off"). If the Position Tool is selected, any action (moving, trimming, etc) will result in an overwrite of existing Clips or the creation of a Gap Clip. This however has a side effect that might be exactly what you want: The Clips on the Timeline won't shift! Yes, you are overwriting Clips but FCPx will not shift Clips along the Timeline that you don't want to be shifted in the first place. Your Clips stay in place.

- **Trimming:** The mouse cursor automatically changes to one of several different icons when moved over specific areas of the Clip to indicate the current trimming mode.

When moved over the left   When moved over the left or right border of a Clip   When moved over the right
end of a Clip (first frame)   that still has footage left to extend   end of a Clip (last frame)

◉ Split Clips

▶ Blade Tool

This trimming command allows you to split a selected Clip in two. Note that this Tool has its built-in Skimming bar so you can see in the Viewer and the SMPTE Reader where you split the Clip. If the Blade is moved over a Clip (active), then it turns black. When moved anywhere else on the Timeline, it changes to a red blade (inactive). Click with a red Blade just moves the Playhead to that position.

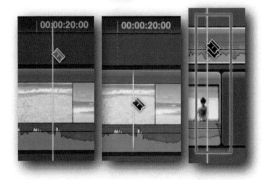

- **Split:** *Click* anywhere on a Clip to split the Clip at that position into two. This works on any Clip, Primary, Storyline or Connected Clip. *Sh+click* splits all Clips across the Timeline at that position. The Cursor tool changes to a double blade.

Moving Clips

Besides trimming Clips in their position, of course you can also move Clip(s) around.

> The Nice Way

▶ **Move any Clip(s) with Pointer Tool**: *Drag* the selection only between existing Clips. Any necessary gap will be closed or Clips moved out of the way.

▶ **Copy any Clip(s) with Pointer Tools**: *Opt+drag* the selected Clip(s). Same dragging behavior.

> The Bully Way

▶ **Move any Clip(s) with Position Tool**: *Drag* the selection freely to any position on the Timeline. Any existing Clips will not change their position but might be (partially) overwritten. Gap Clips will be inserted if necessary.

▶ **Copy any Clip(s) with Position Tool**: *Opt+drag* the selected Clip(s). Again, all the existing Clips will not change their position but might be (partially) overwritten. Gap Clips will be inserted if necessary.

Other Commands

Disable/Enable Clip

You can temporarily disable selected Clips. The following commands toggle the status

- Key Command *V*
- Main Menu: *Clip ➤ Disable/Enable Clip*
- Shortcut Menu: *Disable/Enable*

Clip - Shortcut Menu

Solo Clip

The Solo command disables the audio of every Clip on the Timeline that is not soloed. You can add or remove Clips from the current group of soloed Clips with the special Menu Command *Clip ➤ Add to Soloed Clips.* The following commands toggle the solo status on the selected Clip(s).

- Use the Solo button  in the upper right corner of the Timeline
- Key Command *opt+S*
- Main Menu: *Clip ➤ Solo*

Timeline Buttons

Rename Clip

While you can rename Event Clips directly in the Event Browser, you can also rename the Timeline Clips. You can do it in three different locations.

- Timeline Clip Shortcut Menu: *Rename Clip*
- Timeline Index: *Double-click* the name in the list and type the new name in the entry box
- Inspector: Select the Clip and display the Info tab in the Inspector window. Type the name in the first field

Clip - Shortcut Menu

Timeline Index

Inspector - Info

Connected Clips

There are a few principles regarding Connected Clips that are important when editing Clips.

▶ **Storyline -> Connected**: This is not the official name of the command but it describes the action. You move a Clip from the Primary Storyline up to become a Connected Clip. But if you move the Clip up, then there is no Clip on the Primary Storyline to connect to, right? Unless FCPx just created a Gap Clip, and that is what the Connected Clip now is connected to. This is a perfect example why it's important to look at Gap Clips as actual Clips and not just gaps in the Timeline. You simply *drag* the Clip upwards, or use *sh+drag* to restrict the movement to the vertical position. The official command is *"Lift from Storyline"* ❶, available in the Clip's Shortcut Menu, the Main Menu *Edit ➤ Lift from Storyline* or Key command *opt+cmd+arrow up*.

▶ **Connected -> Storyline**: Basic concept but different direction. The command is *"Overwrite to Primary Storyline"* ❷ and it moves the Connected Clip to the Primary Storyline. However, only the Video content will be overwritten, the audio will be "merged", kind of. The audio track will be expanded and is available as a separate audio track.

➡ Connection Point

Any Clip that is placed as a Connected Clip to an existing Clip on the Primary Storyline (above or below) is connected to that Clip with a *Connection Point*. This is the line that belongs to the Connected Clip. As a default, it is fixed at the first frame of the Connected Clip ❸. You can move the Connected Clip (and the Connecting Point with it) along the timeline to connect it at any position along the Clip on the Primary Storyline.

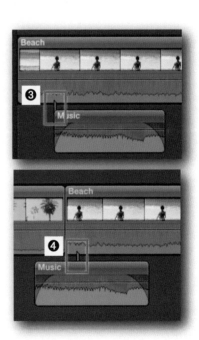

▶ **Move the Connection Point on the Connected Clip**.
Having the Connection Point fixed at the first frame of the Connected Clip is ok under most circumstances. However, there are some situations where this might be a problem. For example, you might have an audio clip as a Connected Clip to the main video clip on the Primary Storyline that needs to start before that video clip (but still connected to that one). In that case, it is necessary to have the Connection Line placed later on the Connected Clip ❹ to connect it to the Clip on the Primary Storyline.
Opt+cmd+click anywhere on the Connected Clip to move the Connection Point to that position.

▶ **Display Connections**
All the Connection Points can be hidden in the Timeline with the checkbox in the Clip Appearance window ❺. Click on the switch in the lower right corner of the Timeline window.

Clip Appearance Window

➡ *Connection Status*

We discussed in this chapter the various techniques how to edit a Clip. However, when editing Clips that are "connected", the rules are different.

First question is, which Clip are we editing, the Connected Clip or the Clip on the Primary Storyline that has a Connected Clip attached to it.

Edit Connected Clip

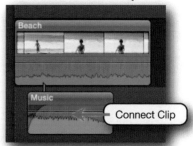

🔘 Edit Connected Clip

You can freely edit the Connected Clip, move it, trim it, etc. It doesn't affect any other Clip, just the placement of the Clip itself. Please note that the Connection Point might be affected by some edit procedures. For example, trimming the beginning of the Clip will move the Connection Point with it. However this doesn't affect its relative position to the parent Clip on the Primary Storyline.

Edit Primary Storyline Clip

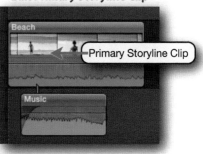

🔘 Edit Clip on Primary Storyline with an attached Connected Clip

Editing the parent Clip on the Primary Storyline is more critical. This could move the Connected Clips and eventually result in "out of sync" Clips. There are two status that determine the outcome of the edit.

▶ Connected (default)

> This is the default behavior and when FCPx was first introduced, it was the big advantage of Connected Clips. They latch on to the Clip on the Primary Storyline and when you move that Clip on the Primary Storyline, all the Connected Clips will move with it and stay in sync (i.e. audio, sound fx, overlays, etc). However, I pointed out already in the previous sections that there are some dangers you have to be aware of.
>
> Deleting a Clip on the Primary Storyline will also delete any of its Connected Clips!

▶ Disconnected 🚫

> This status overwrites the default status of having a Connected Clip always move with its parent Clip on the Primary Storyline. In a situation where you want the Connected Clip keep its timeline position regardless of any changes to its parent Clip on the Primary Storyline (move it, trim it, delete it). It will disconnect from the parent Clip and "hold on" to its timeline position. To perform this edit, hold down the Grave Accent (`) key, the one above the tab key, also referred to as the "Tilde" key (~). A special icon appears to indicate that you are editing in this special mode.
>
> Deleting a Clip on the Primary Storyline now will NOT delete its Connected Clips. Any Clips on the Primary Storyline move to the left to fill the gap (Magnetic Timeline). If there are no Clips on the Primary Storyline to connect to, then FCPx creates a Gap Clip in that place.

Move Clip	**Trim Clip**	**Delete Clip**

🔘 Edit both Clips

Selecting both, the Clip on the Primary Storyline and its Connected Clip(s), lets you move or duplicate (or delete) them together while keeping their connection intact.

I touched the topic of Clip Properties before but, especially in the context of editing in the Timeline, it is very important to understand what is affecting what at what level. Here is the underlying concept again with a different diagram.

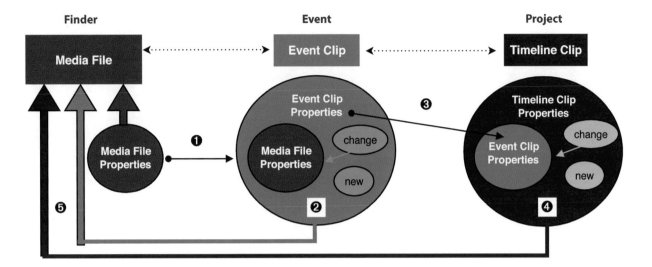

❶ You import a Media File into an Event. An Event Clip is created in the Event that is linked to that Media File. The Event Clip inherits the original Properties of the Media File. It is like a one time "lookup".

❷ The Event Clip Properties can now be edited in the Inspector. You can change the inherited Properties and add new ones.

❸ Now the Event Clip gets dragged onto the Project Timeline. A Timeline Clip is created on the Timeline that is linked to the Event Clip. The Timeline Clip now inherits the Properties of the Event Clip. Part of the Properties is the location of the Source Media File that the Event Clip is linked to. Again, this is a one time lookup.
It is very important to understand why this copy process of the Properties is a one time "lookup" at the moment when the Timeline Clip is created. Any changes made in the Event Clip later on are not reflected in the Timeline Clip.

❹ The Timeline Clip Properties can now be edited in the Inspector. Those changes are unique to that Timeline Clip. Any Clip that is placed on the Timeline carries its individual Properties that can be edited. Every time you drag an Event Clip from the Event Browser to the Timeline or copy a Timeline Clip on the Timeline, you create a new Timeline Clip. Each of those "new" Timeline Clips has its own Properties that can be edited independently in the Inspector.

❺ If you play back the original Media File in the Finder (with QuickView), its own playback Properties apply. When you play back the Event Clip, then any playback instruction stored in the Event Clip Properties will apply when playing back the Media File. (i.e. play at -6dB). When you play back the Timeline Clip, any playback instruction stored in the Timeline Clip Properties will apply when playing back the Media File. (i.e. play with reverb and change the color tone of the video). Of course all those instructions are non-destructive playback instructions. The Media File stays untouched. Please note that his model doesn't take the concept of rendering into account (which I cover in the second book).

Editing the Properties for the Event Clip or the Timeline Clip is straight forward. You have the Inspector open *cmd+4* and select the Clip. The Inspector displays the information from whatever Clip is selected and you go ahead and make any necessary changes in the Inspector.

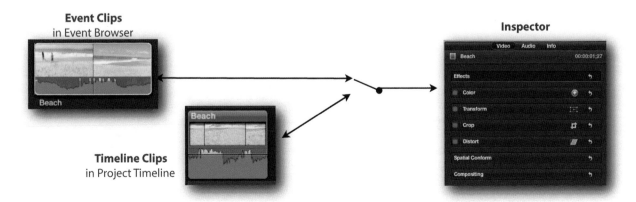

The concept of applying playback parameters is very simple and easy. Every Clip has its own Property List (kind of its DNA). That list carries:

- ▶ **Info:** General information about the Clip, its whole identity.
- ▶ **Video + Audio**: Playback parameters that have instructions on how to play back the audio and video portion of the Clip. These are the non-destructive playback instructions for the original Media File when played back as we have seen in the previous diagram. Those playback instructions are grouped in Modules in the Inspector.

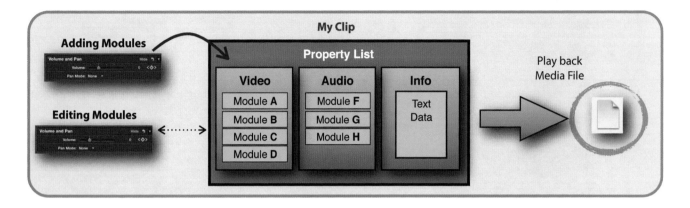

There are two kinds of Modules:

- ▶ **Default Modules**: These Modules are already available in the Inspector and cannot be removed (only bypassed).
- ▶ **Effects Modules**: These are Modules only available for the Timeline Clips (not the Event Clips). Those effects can be added (*drag* or *double-click*) to the Timeline Clip from the *Media Browser* window (open with *cmd+5*).

➡ *Module GUI*

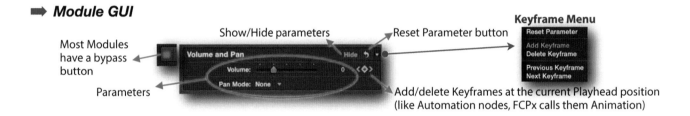

Here are the Inspector's Property Lists with the default Modules for the Video and Audio tab. Please note that the Timeline Clips have a few more Modules plus the Effects Module. The Effects Module is a display section that groups all the Effects Modules inside like a container. It functions as an FX Rack where you can re-arrange the order of the FX. The FX itself might even have its own separate GUI.

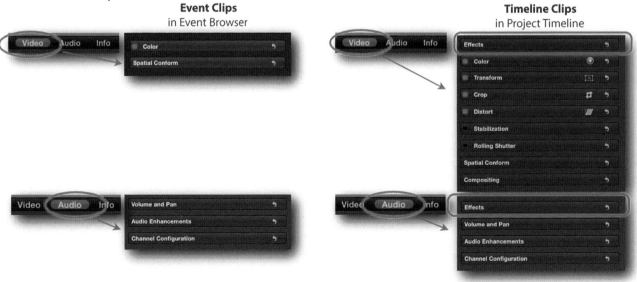

We've already covered many of the new concepts in FCPx. For example, FCPx being a non document-based application, the single window GUI, the Event-Project relationship, Primary Storyline and Connected Clips, or the Magnetic Timeline. I also mentioned already that the audio portion of a video clip is now part of the single (combined) Clip.

In regards to audio handling in FCPx, this is only the "tip of the iceberg". There are fundamentally different concepts, not only compared to FCP7 but compared to video editor applications in general. Needles to say, they require a rethinking of common workflows but have the potential of providing more powerful workflows in the end.

New Concept

Here are the two most important changes regarding audio in FCPx.

Single (combined) Clip

The diagram below again shows a Video Clip, an Image Clip and an Audio Clip and how they look in the Event Browser and on the Timeline.

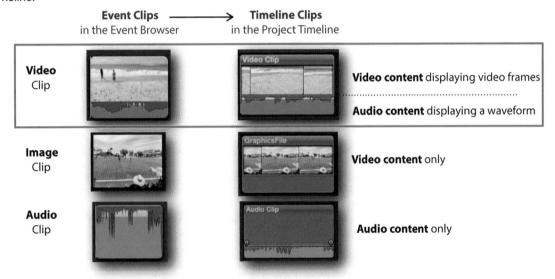

While an Audio Clip contains only the audio track(s) and an Image Clip contains only the video track (one video frame), a Video Clip on the other hand, can include both portions, the video track and the audio track(s). This new concept comes with new editing techniques that we'll explore in a minute.

Object-based Audio (No More Mixer)

The other big change is the elimination of the audio mixer. However, this is not just the removal of a specific feature. There is a bigger picture behind it. It is the result of a fundamentally different concept concerning the way FCPx deals with audio in general.

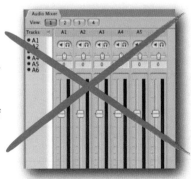

Audio in FCPx is not based on the traditional concept of a mixing consoles and signal routing anymore, it is based on objects, attributes and metadata. Another sign that the overall architecture of FCPx has become more like a database. I will cover the aspect of metadata in the second book "Final Cut Pro X - The Details". In this chapter, we will learn what it means to treat audio not as an audio signal but as an object.

Now lets have a closer look at those changes.

Single (combined) Clip

In the Chapter about Clips and Editing, we treated a Video Clip as one single clip, one single object that contained the video and audio portion. This had the advantage that all editing commands (trimming, moving, copying) were applied to that one single Clip.

However that Video Clip is actually a container that contains two Clips, a Video Clip and an Audio Clip. They are just combined into one which allows for more efficient editing. Although not used in this context, the proper term would be a "Compound Clip", a Clip which contains other Clips, a topic of the second book.

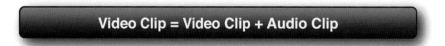

Video Clip = Video Clip + Audio Clip

While there are big advantages when editing only one (combined) Clip, there are occasions when you want to edit the video and audio portion of a Video Clip separately. The good news is that FCPx provides that option, actually more than one option.

Display Options

Here is an overview of the different ways a Video Clip can be displayed in the Timeline. Please note that those display options are only available for the Timeline Clip. An Event Clip can only be displayed in its combined form

The one exception is the command "Open in Timeline" which is an additional display option that I cover in the Compound Clip chapter.

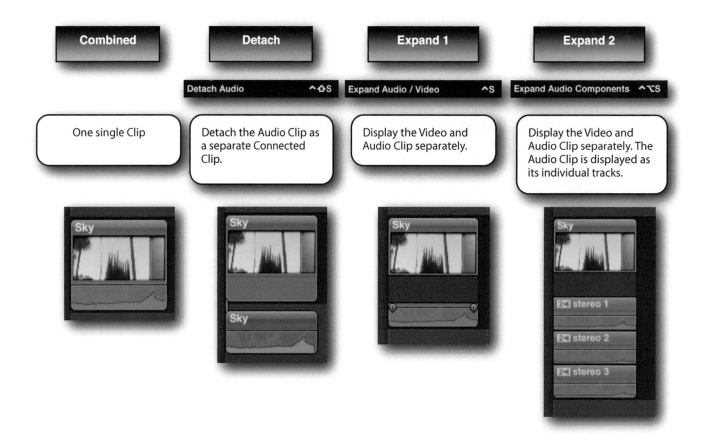

➡ Detach Audio

Use any of the following commands:

- Main Menu *Clip ➤ Detach Audio*
- Shortcut Menu *Detach Audio*
- Key Command *sh+ctr+S*

This is the more radical approach which breaks the Clip up into a separate Video and Audio Clip. Both Clips will have the same name. This command cannot be reversed later, only with the Undo command.

If the combined Clip is located on the Primary Storyline, then the new Video Clip stays on the Primary Storyline and the Audio Clip will become a Connected Clip. If the combined Clip is already a Connected Clip, then both new Clips end up being Connected Clips, connected to their original Clip on the Primary Storyline.

➡ Expand (Collapse) Audio/Video

Use any of the following commands:

- Main Menu *Clip ➤ Expand (Collapse) Audio/Video*
- Shortcut Menu *Expand (Collapse) Audio/Video*
- Key Command *ctr+S*
- *Double-click* on the waveform

This command also breaks the Video and Audio Clip apart but only visually. This is just a pure display feature that can be toggled with the same command. Please note that the expanded Clip is still one unit indicated by the dark area that connects the video and audio portion. Also, the audio portion still has the blue color which hints at a video Clip and not a separate (green) Audio Clip.

➡ Expand (Collapse) Audio Components

Use any of the following commands:

- Main Menu *Clip ➤ Expand (Collapse) Audio Components*
- Shortcut Menu *Expand (Collapse) Audio Components*
- Key Command *ctr+opt+S*

This display option is just a variation of the "Expand Audio/Video" command. Now the audio portion is broken up into its individual audio tracks. For example, if the audio contains a stereo track, then it will display only a single stereo track but if it contains two mono tracks, then both mono tracks will be displayed as what looks like two separate Audio Clips. The example on the right displays a 5.1 surround mix that is configured as three stereo tracks.

FCPx calls those audio tracks *Audio Components*. The understanding of those Audio Components (or audio tracks) is very important when it comes to mixing as we will see later in this chapter.

Shortcut Menu: Timeline Clip

The Clip Menu and the Shortcut Menu contain all the commands for those options.

The Clip Menu has an additional command "*Break Apart Clip Items*". This has a similar affect as the Detach Audio command creating separate Connected Clips. Here, FCPx looks at the original source media files and creates individual Clips for each track (video and audio) that are part of the media file.

Main Menu: Clip

Editing Expanded Clips

When editing a Video Clip, all the trimming commands are applied to the video and audio portion as one. But sometimes it is necessary to treat them individually. Detach the Audio would work because it creates two independent Clips, but that defeats the advantage of having a combined clip in the first place.

Expanding the Clip keeps the video and audio portion attached together while still providing separate trimming and editing.

➡ *Trimming*

◉ Expand Audio/Video

Here is a simple example how to trim the audio portion separately from the video portion of a Clip.

❶ The first Clip (Sky) is expanded. Please note that the Primary Storyline is getting stretched vertically to accommodate the expanded Clip.

❷ Here I trimmed only the audio portion extending it to the right so it plays longer than the video portion.

❸ Here I expanded also the second Clip (Beach) and trimmed its audio portion to start earlier creating an audio overlap between the two Clips. Please note that the Primary Storyline stretches even further. Any overlapping section will be displayed stacked on top of each other in a very clean visual way.

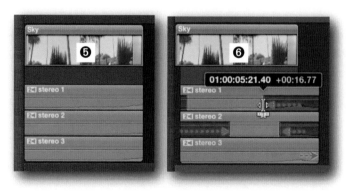

Reset

Use the Menu Command *Clip ➤ Clear Audio/Video Split* ❹ to reset the audio portion back to the same length as the video portion of the selected Clip.

◉ Expanded Audio Components

With the *Expand Audio/Video* command you can also trim the video and audio portion independently. However, you can take it one step further when using clips containing multichannel audio. When you display the individual audio Components inside a Video with the *Expand Audio Components* command, you can trim each individual Component against the video and against each other.

❺ The Clip is expanded displaying its three audio Components, here they represent three stereo channels. Visually, they indicate that they are still part of one combined Video Clip.

❻ Please note the details in the interface. Each Component has an upper lane and a lower lane. The upper lane displays the name of the Component and the number of audio channels 2◀ for that Component. The upper lanes always span from the earliest to the latest edit point of the (trimmed) audio portion. The lower lane of each Component is the one that can be trimmed. Position the cursor slightly to the right of the right border or slightly to the left of the left border to get the trimming tool ▐▌. If you drag inside the lane, the cursor changes to the Range tool ▣.

➡ Advanced Trimming

You can take the trimming techniques even further in the Expand Audio Components view.

❶ This Clip contains two audio Components, each one carrying a mono channel (mono1, mono 2)

❷ As we have seen in the previous example, you can trim the beginning and end of each Component individually. In this example, the first Component comes in later and stops earlier.

❸ Moving the mouse over a Component changes the cursor to the Range tool 🔲 that lets you *drag* a Range selection on that Audio Component.

❹ Using the *Disable* Command (Shortcut Menu, Clip Menu or Key Command *V*) disables only that selected Range. The Component now shows that muted section as a dimmed area.

❺ You can mark multiple selection with the Range Tool on any Component and disable those sections very quickly to mute parts of specific Audio Components.

❻ You can also use the Range tool to mark a section and quickly change the level just for that section on that channel by *dragging* the volume automation line up or down. This creates keyframes (part of the Audio Automation I cover in the Automation chapter of book 2).

These trimming techniques for multichannel audio are very quick and efficient. Everything is contained in a single Clip. You just Show the Audio Components, do the edit and Collapse the Audio Component. A nice, fast and clean workflow that would be quite labor intensive in FCP7.

➡ Parameter Editing

I covered the concept of applying effects to a Clip already in the Editing Chapter: Select the Clip, select the Parameter (or add a new effects parameter) in the Inspector and adjust the value. This is the basic concept of editing individual Objects which now also applied to audio editing and mixing. Here is the big advantage.

❼ **Single Clip**: With one Clip, the Object is one single item (the audio portion of the clip) and any edit applied to that Clip will be applied to all its containing audio channels equally.

❽ **Expanded Audio Component Clip**: With the Audio Component expanded, each Component is a separate Object and any edits can be applied now to those individual Objects. For example apply some equalizer or other effects to only one channel or pan the individual Components differently (center, left, right).

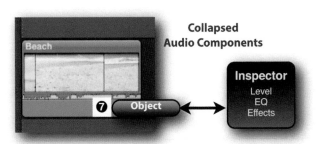

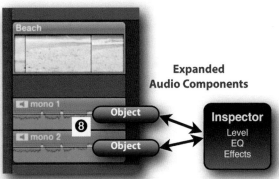

In the next section, we'll find out more about this object-based audio editing.

Object-based Audio

Apple made a bold move and eliminated the concept of tracks in FCPx replacing it with the Primary Storyline. Besides messing up some common workflows that editors are used to, this change creates a big headache on the audio side too. In the audio world (Pro Tools, Logic Pro), everything is still based on tracks and it was the common "hand shake" between the video and audio world along with established file exchange formats.

Audio clips were placed on audio tracks in the video app that were connected to mixer channels to do basic audio mixing in the video project.

The various audio clips could be placed on predetermined tracks (Dialog, Ambient, Foley, Music, etc) to get everything organized better. Those tracks could be handed over to the ProTools guy for mixing or could be processed with the companion app, Soundtrack Pro.

Now all this is gone. However, along with the shift from "audio signals" to "audio objects", FCPx introduced a new powerful feature called *"Roles"*. These changes require some rethinking of conventional workflows but offer new functionality that wasn't possible before.

Inspector is the new Mixer

To better understand the audio concept in FCPx, think of it as a transition from an analog to a digital mindset. The analog way was track-based where you had tracks (on a video machine or an audio multitrack machine) that carried the signal. The signal from the machine output was routed through a mixer where you balanced the signal and inserted FX for further signal processing. The mixed output signal was then sent out to the destination like speakers or another recording device.

This concept is simulated in virtually all DAWs (Digital Audio Workstations). Under the hood however, there is no signal that is carried from one output to the other. Everything is based on computer code with zeros and ones, objects and addresses, etc.

FCPx now takes it to the next level. Instead of simulating an analog mixing model with digital "tools", it stays in the "digital mindset" when it comes to editing and mixing audio.

The individual audio signal becomes an Object that represents an audio channel

An audio signal in the analog domain is usually represented by a track on a tape machine (were you record that signal) or a Channel Strip on a mixing board (where you process that signal). In the digital domain that audio signal is represented by an Audio Channel which is embedded in the Source Media File (video file or audio file). And those individual Audio Channels are the Objects that we are editing with the Inspector. The Inspector displays the Parameters and Attributes of a selected Object (level, pan, effect, channel configuration) and changing those parameters requires adjusting their values in the Inspector.

The Inspector becomes - **Your New Mixing Board.**

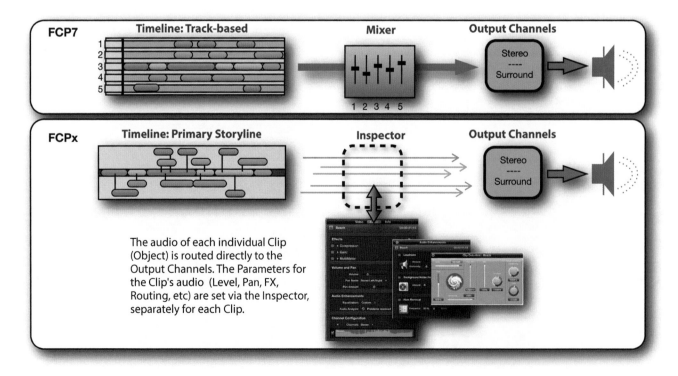

The audio of each individual Clip (Object) is routed directly to the Output Channels. The Parameters for the Clip's audio (Level, Pan, FX, Routing, etc) are set via the Inspector, separately for each Clip.

Inspector

Now let's have a look at our new mixer, the Inspector, and see how that thing could possibly replace an audio mixer.

The basic procedure of mixing an audio track is now the same as editing an object in a computer application like Photoshop, a word processor or a layout application.

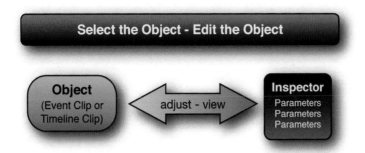

☑ **Select the Object** (or multiple objects)

This means, selecting a Clip first. This could be either an Event Clip or a Timeline Clip. On a Timeline Clip you can even select individual Audio Components in the expanded view as we have seen in the previous section.

☑ **Open the Inspector**

We discussed earlier that the Inspector is a special window used in many applications. It lets you view and adjust the parameters of a selected Object.

☑ **View Parameter Values**

Having the Inspector window open while selecting different Objects, lets you view the values of their parameters.

☑ **Adjust Parameter Values**

Adjusting the values of the available parameters in the Inspector will apply those changes to the currently selected Object(s). Always make sure to know what Object (what Clip or Component) is the selected one.

If any Object is selected that has audio content (Video Clip with audio content or Audio Clip), then the Inspector will have an Audio tab that lists all the available audio parameters. The parameters are grouped in Modules. A Timeline Clip has an additional Module not available on an Event Clip. This is the Effects Module that functions like an Effects Rack where you can add additional audio effect modules to further process the selected audio channels.

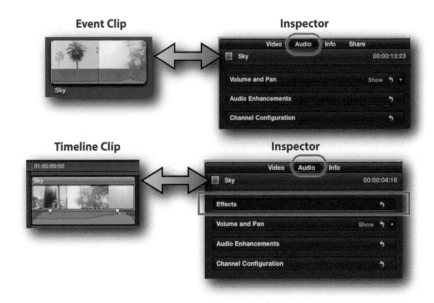

☻ **Event Clip**

- ▶ Volume and Pan
- ▶ Audio Enhancements
- ▶ Channel Configuration

☻ **Timeline Clip**

- ▶ Effects
- ▶ Volume and Pan
- ▶ Audio Enhancements
- ▶ Channel Configuration

➡ Show/Hide Parameters

Hide Parameters - Show Parameters

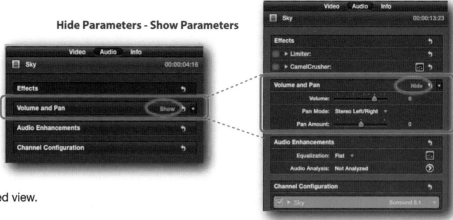

Double-click on the Module header to expand it and display all the Parameters inside. Moving the mouse over the header will also display a blue "Show" button that can be clicked on too.

If expanded, that button now displays "Hide" when moved over the header. Click on it or *double-click* the header to close the expanded view.

➡ Keep in mind

Whenever you are in the Inspector, viewing and/or adjusting Parameters, be aware of two things:

- 💡 What Object is selected?
- 💡 Is the selected Object an Event Clip or a Timeline Clip?

This sounds trivial but keep in mind:

- ▶ Of course you don't want to change values in the Inspector and find out later that you edited the wrong Clip. Always keep an eye on what Clip(s) is selected.
- ▶ You can select multiple Clips and change their Parameters simultaneously.
- ▶ Selecting a Clip will add a yellow border around it. Now you know that it is selected and if the Inspector is visible, it will display the Parameters of the selected Clip. However, if you want to edit those Parameters, you have to select the Inspector. This changes the key focus from the Timeline (or Event Browser) to the Inspector. The yellow border that indicates the selected Clip(s) changes its color to gray. Be aware of the subtle difference when looking for that visual feedback.
- ▶ Another thing to remember. Event Clips and Timeline Clips have their own properties. Moving an Event Clip to the Timeline creates an independent Timeline Clip that inherits the Event Clip properties. All subsequent changes in the Timeline Clip do not affect its parent Event Clip. Same thing when copying (duplicating) Timeline Clips on the Timeline itself. This creates a new independent Timeline Clip. So be aware of where you make audio adjustments and why. For example, if Event Clips need some basic treatment (channel assignment, level was to low or too hot), those can be made to the Event Clips so when it is time to drag them onto the timeline, those parameters will be carried over.

    - • *Advanced Tip*: Although you cannot add Effects to an Event Clip because the Inspector doesn't show the Effects Module, you can open the Event Clip in the Timeline with the "*Open in Timeline*" command. This opens up tremendous opportunities in FCPx. More about that in the second book "Final Cut Pro X - The Details".

Clip selected
Window has key focus

Clip selected
Window has not key focus

➡ Additional Controls

The Inspector is the place where you view and edit all the parameters. However, the Timeline Clip itself also has two areas where you can view and edit Parameters. Those Parameters are corresponding with the Parameters displayed in the Inspector and are updated on either side.

- 💡 **Volume display**: This lane displays the level for the clip volume ❶ including any Keyframes plus Fade Handles ❷. Please note that the two Fade Handles are unique to the Timeline Clip and are NOT shown in the Inspector!
- 💡 **Audio Animation Lane**: Animation lanes (Show/Hide Audio Animation) display any Parameter as a function over time plus any available Keyframes ❹. See the Animation chapter for details.

Let's look at the 4 Inspector Modules in detail to see what Audio Parameters we can adjust and how we adjust them.

- **Effects**: This Module is like an Effects Rack that can be loaded up with effect plugins.
- **Volume and Pan**: The Module that sets the overall level and the pan setting for stereo and surround.
- **Audio Enhancements**: A few built-in effects for quick audio adjustments.
- **Channel Configuration**: The new output routing module.

Below is a diagram that lists the Inspector Modules as Components in a conventional audio signal flow. This is just a model to show what elements affect the Clip's audio before it reaches the destination, a speaker or an exported media file.

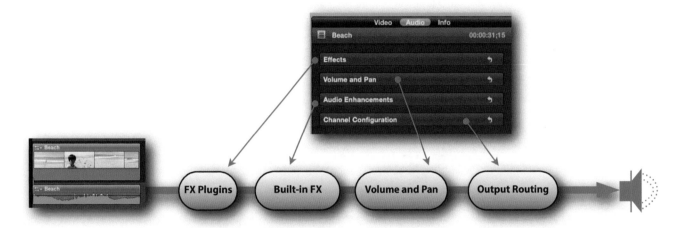

Most of the Modules in the Audio Inspector are easy to understand like Volume, Equalizer and other Effects. The last one however, Channel Configuration, is arguably the most important one and easy to overlook. Failing to understand the concept behind it could result in some unpleasant surprises. So let's start look into that one first.

Channel Configuration

How can this Module be so important and complicated? It has only one control bar.

That one bar displays the following items:

- ☑ A checkbox
- ☑ A disclosure triangle
- ☑ The Name of the selected (displayed) Clip
- ☑ A popup menu

The color code tells you if the audio is part of a Video Clip (blue) or Audio Clip (green)

Channels

Here is how the Channel Configuration fits into the "big picture" of FCPx.

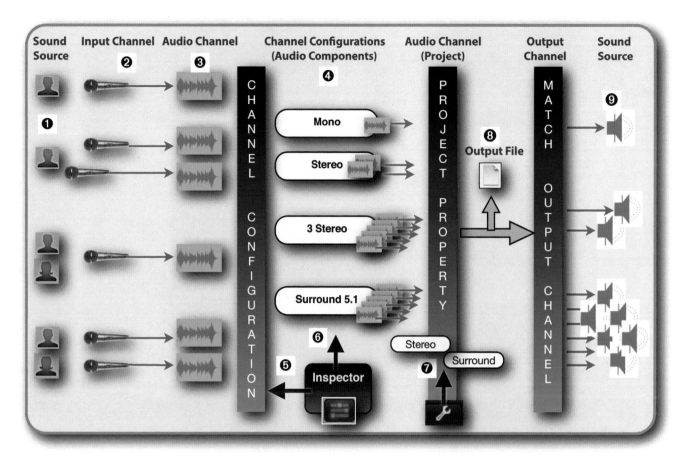

❶ The Sound Source is the original audio signal you want to record. This can be one signal (one actor) or many signals (group of actors).

❷ The Input Channel is the discrete signal that you are recording. As you can see in the diagram, the number of Sound Sources can be different from the number of Input Channels. You can record two sources with one mic (one Input Channel) or one Source with multiple mics (multiple Input Channels). For example, recording an actor with the camera mic and boom mic.

❸ Each recorded Input Channel creates a discrete Audio Channel represented by a single waveform.

❹ Those discrete Audio Channels can be grouped as a specific Channel Configuration. Two channels can be grouped into one single Stereo component or two Mono components. Six channels can be grouped into a single 5.1 Surround component or grouped into three stereo components. You could even configure the six channels into six mono components, one component per channel. As you can see, the process of the Channel Configuration is just an instruction about how to group the discrete audio channels.

❺ The Inspector is the tool where you select one of the available Channel Configurations.

❻ The Inspector can now also apply any signal processing to individual Audio Components just by selecting that Audio Component instead of the entire Clip itself. For example, if you configure a 5.1 recording as six mono components, then you can edit each channel individually, applying more bass to the FX channel or a special EQ to the center channel.

❼ Independent from these Channel Configurations, set individually for each Clip, is the Audio Channel configuration for the Project (like a Master Track). This is part of the Project Properties, set when you create a new Project or changed later at any time. It can be set to either Stereo (two channels) or Surround (six channels). The Audio Components of a Clip are "running through" the Pan Parameter which determines how each Audio Component is routed to the Project's Audio Channels.

❽ The Output File, created when exporting the Project, inherits the format, set in the Project Properties (Stereo or Surround).

❾ This is the last stage where the Project's Audio Channels (stereo or surround) are automatically matched to the available Output Channels on your hardware. For example, you might be monitoring through the mono speaker or stereo speaker on your computer or through a surround sound setup hooked up to an external audio interface. This process enables you to listen to a stereo speaker even if you are working on a Project configured for surround.

Now let's have a closer look at the Channel Configuration to make sure we fully understand that section. Especially how it relates to the Audio Components.

Here are the four important elements:

Source Media File

This is the file with audio content that the Event Clip or Timeline Clip is referenced to. The file could be either created straight from a recording (i.e. from the camera) or come from a file export (mixdown) through an application.

Discrete Audio Channels

The first question about the audio is, how many discrete channels does the audio carry. Is it just one channel from a single microphone or two channels from a stereo mic. Maybe the file is a surround sound mix that carries six or even more discrete channels.

Channel Configuration

Channel Configurations are the different ways of grouping those discrete channels together. Those groups are often called tracks, but FCPx use the term *Audio Components*. A Media File stores its discrete channels in a specific format, its (default) Channel Configuration.

Audio Components

A Channel Configuration contains one or more Audio Components (Tracks) which itself contain the discrete Audio Channels. For example, a file that carries two Channels (from a stereo mix recording) could configure them as one single stereo track (one Audio Component) carrying both channels on that one track. An alternative is to configure it as two mono tracks (two Audio Components), each one carrying one channel.

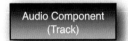

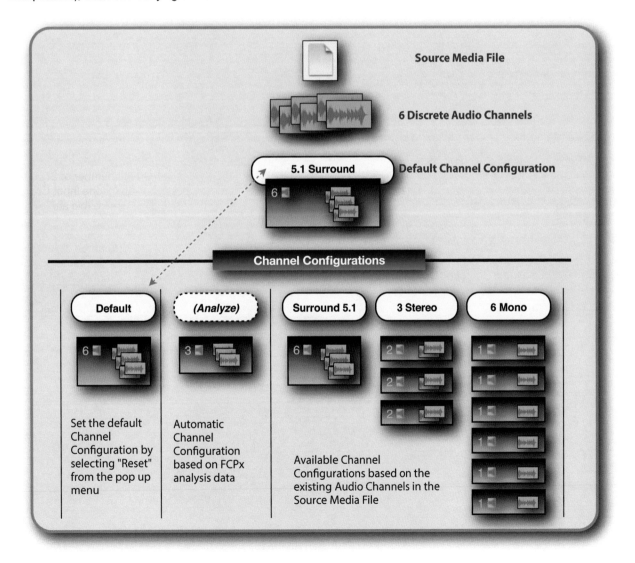

Those previous diagrams might need some time to digest. However, it is important to understand those concepts if you want to control the audio part of your Project and try to avoid "surprises" regarding the audio. (By the way, this is just the foundation. I haven't talked about Metadata and Roles yet.)

Here is a simplified diagram that summarizes the importance of the Channel Configuration.

The potential misunderstanding about the Channel Configuration is that it could be compared to the output routing in a traditional audio signal flow. After all, FCPx lists it as the last Module in the Audio Inspector. However, the Channel Configuration determines the output routing AND the input routing. It takes the available Input Channels and provides different options on how to group those channels together as Audio Components. This selection then determines how the signal gets routed to the available Output Channels in conjunction with the pan control.

Everything centers around the Channel Configuration

With that understanding, let's look at the user interface of the Channel Configuration Module.

❶ The popup menu provides a list of all the available Channel Configurations. These are the of options how to group the available Channels. Because the available options depend on the channels that are available in the source media file, the items in the list vary with different Clips.

❷ Selecting any item on the list changes to that Channel Configuration.

❸ The *Reset* command switches back to the default channel configuration from the source media file. The Reset button in the Module header has the same effect. Be aware that this also removes any settings applied to the Audio Components.

❹ The disclosure triangle on the top reveals all the individual Audio Components in that configuration displaying their waveforms. Please note that this is the waveform of the Audio Component. If that Audio Component contains only one Channel, then you will see the waveform of that Channel. If an Audio Component contains two or more Channels, then the waveform displays the sum of those Channels. The waveform is always zoomed so it is displaying the whole length of the Clip.

❺ You can rename the Audio Components. Click on the name and type into the entry box.

❻ The checkboxes next to each Audio Component mute only the channels of that Audio Component. A muted Audio Component is dimmed. The checkbox on the top lets you mute the whole audio portion of the Clip. It displays a minus button 🔲 to indicate if some components are muted and some not.

❼ If an Audio Component includes more than one channel, then the speaker icon next to the checkbox will include the number of channels.

❽ Clip Skimming is always active (scrubbing along an Audio Component). Please be aware that although the Skimming bar is always visible, you only hear the sound if Audio Skimming is activated in the View Menu (not necessarily with the Audio Skimming button

🎚️ (see the Playhead section for details about the somewhat confusing Skimming implementation).

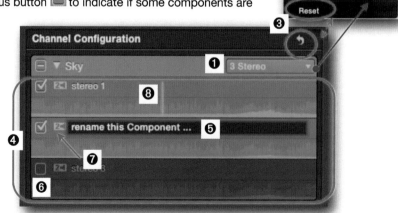

Here are examples of three Clips based on three different source media files with different audio channels and therefore different Channel Configurations to choose from..

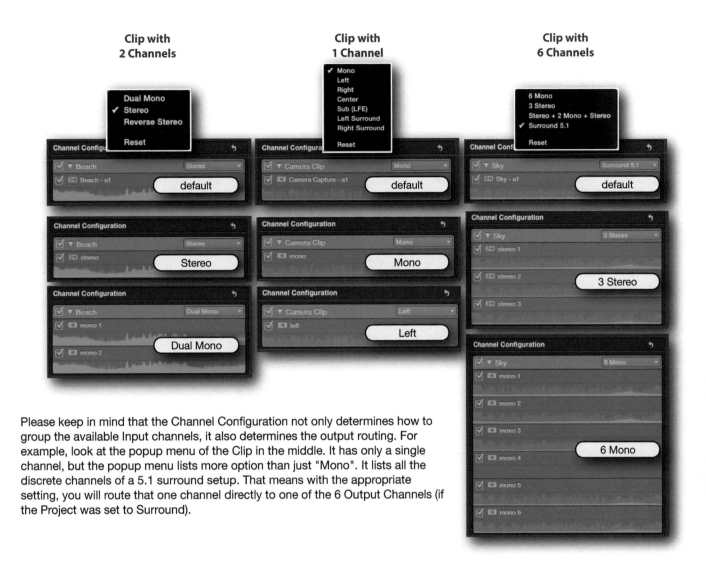

Please keep in mind that the Channel Configuration not only determines how to group the available Input channels, it also determines the output routing. For example, look at the popup menu of the Clip in the middle. It has only a single channel, but the popup menu lists more option than just "Mono". It lists all the discrete channels of a 5.1 surround setup. That means with the appropriate setting, you will route that one channel directly to one of the 6 Output Channels (if the Project was set to Surround).

➡ *Analyze and Fix*

There is one more element that has to be taken into consideration regarding the Channel Configuration. Remember the chapter about Importing Media. FCPx has a feature that automatically analyzes the audio portion of a Clip. This can be done during the import of the source media file or anytime later with a command from the Shortcut Menu. It can remove any channels that have no audio signal and also set the Channel Configuration to "Dual Mono" or "Stereo" depending on the analysis.

There are three types of the Channel Configurations:

💡 Default

This is the default audio Channel Configuration as it is stored with the source media file. Click *Reset* in the popup menu to switch to that one.

💡 Analyzed and Fixed

This is the Channel Configuration that is determined by the automatic analysis.

💡 Custom

These are the Channel Configuration that are available from the popup menu in the Channel Configuration Module.

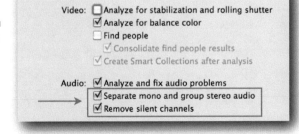

➡ *Output Routing - Channel Matching*

We saw already earlier on the big diagram that even after the Channel Configuration, there are two more stages that affect the channel routing.

- 🔊 Audio Channel configuration of the Project (Surround / Stereo)
- 🔊 Output Channel configuration of your hardware (Speakers)

Please note that Event Clips and Timeline Clips are different regarding those routing steps.

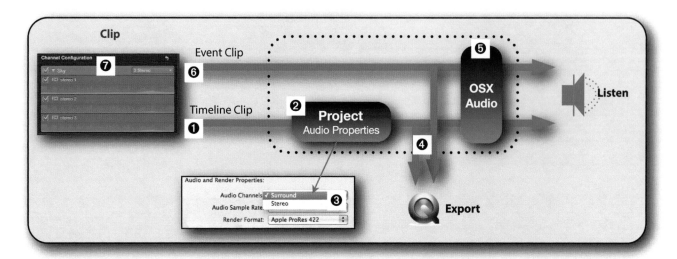

🔊 The **Timeline Clips** ❶ of a Project have to match first against Audio Channel settings in the Project Properties ❷. You have to set a Project to stereo or surround ❸ when you first create a Project (can be changed later). This setting determines the Exported File ❹.
However, when you select surround and play back a surround clip, you still won't hear surround if you're stuck with stereo speakers. The OSX output channel setting ❺ (available speakers) requires a second step to match the channels.

🔊 The **Event Clips** ❻ are not affected by the Project Properties ❸. That means if you export ❹ an Event Clip, its output file format is only determined by the Clip's Channel Configuration ❼.
Monitoring the Clip through your speakers however, still requires the extra step to match the channels to the systems output setting ❺.

Here are the conversion (matching) rules:

- ▶ **Stereo --> surround**: The left and right channels are matched to the left and right channels of the surround channels.
- ▶ **Surround --> stereo**: The surround channels are mixed down to stereo (left and right channel).
- ▶ **Stereo or surround --> mono**: Both are mixed down to mono (one channel).

Audio Component Editing

We discussed already the powerful feature of applying signal processing to individual Audio Components. Instead of selecting the Clip itself and adjusting the parameters in the Inspector, you can Expand the Audio Components on the Timeline Clip, select any components, and adjust the parameters in the Inspector just for that Audio Component.

If an Audio Component is selected in a Timeline Clip

Channel Configuration ↩

Audio Channels Configuration is unavailable for the selected clips

We understand now that the Channel Configuration Module in the Audio Inspector applies to the entire Clip. This is where you determine the structure of the audio channels for that Clip.
Therefore it makes no sense to select an Audio Component in the Timeline Clip and modify the Channel Configuration Module. The Inspector realizes that too and displays that note if an Audio Component is selected.

Volume and Pan

The Volume and Pan Module controls only two parameters, Volume and Pan.

➡ *Volume*

The Volume Parameter has only one slider and a value display/entry box. For Timeline Clips, the slider corresponds to the volume line in the Clips volume lane. The Module displays Keyframes if they are programmed for that Clip. The displayed waveform in the Clip is the result "after" the volume settings, so you can see if your level is too low or to high (blue-yellow-red indication).

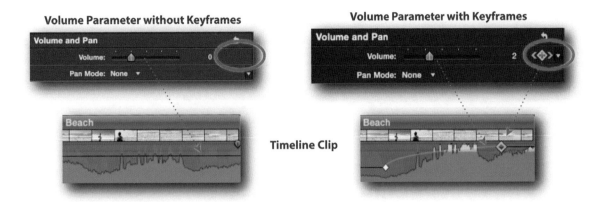

Adjust Volume

There are multiple ways to adjust the Volume for a selected Timeline Clip (only the first three are available for Event Clips):

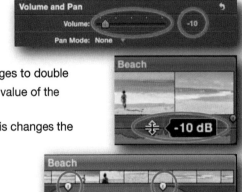

► Move the volume slider in the Inspector.

► Enter a dB value into the value box next to the slider in the Inspector.

► *Drag* the dB value up and down when two little up and down arrows appear while you move the mouse over.

► *Drag* the Volume line on the Timeline Clip's waveform lane. The cursor changes to double arrows when the mouse is on the line. A little black window displays the dB value of the Volume line.

► Use the Main Menu *Modify ➤ Volume ➤ Up* or *Modify ➤ Volume ➤ Down*. This changes the volume by 1dB increments and can be used for multiple selected Clips.

► Use the Key Command *ctr+=* or *ctr+-*. This changes the volume by 1dB increments and can be used for multiple selected Clips.

► Fade Handles: Technically, this also belongs to volume adjustments. Remember, the waveform doesn't respond to the fade settings. I discuss the details about Fade Handles in the Automation chapter.

Crossfade Type

A crossfade is another element that adjusts the volume of your Clip. In FCP7 an audio clip is a separate clip and any crossfade must be created separately for the video and the audio clip. In FCPx a video clip also contains its audio content so if you apply a crossfade to a video clip, the audio is crossfaded too. However, you can adjust the crossfade separately by selecting the Transition. This allows you to access the Parameters in the Inspector.

You can set the crossfade type from the popup menu separately for the Fade In and Fade Out.

➡ *Pan*

The second section on the Module, the Pan settings, has only one popup menu. A very powerful one:

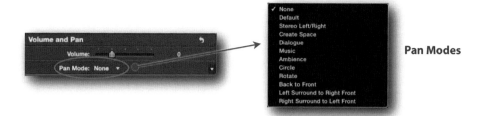

Pan Modes

The popup menu gets very complex because the effect of each selection depends on the settings in the Channel Configuration Module that we discussed earlier. In addition to that, the Pan Module functions differently depending on the Audio Properties of the Project. As you can see, I placed the Channel Configuration Module before the Pan Module!

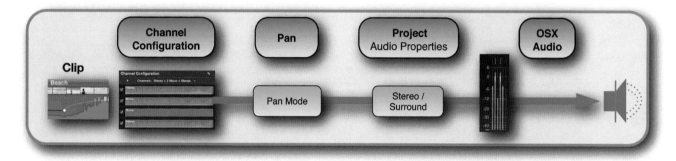

Every time the channels of the various components don't match (i.e. output has 2 channels, input has 6 channels) FCPx has to perform some intelligent channel re-assignment to match the channels.

Example:

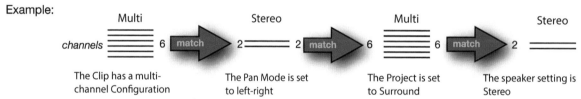

All the different Pan Mode Presets in the menu can be grouped into three types. You can distinguish the type by what controls are provided:

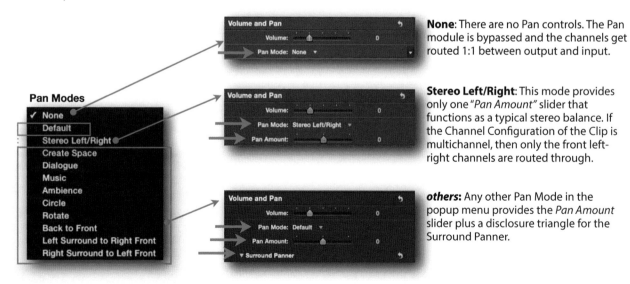

None: There are no Pan controls. The Pan module is bypassed and the channels get routed 1:1 between output and input.

Stereo Left/Right: This mode provides only one *"Pan Amount"* slider that functions as a typical stereo balance. If the Channel Configuration of the Clip is multichannel, then only the front left-right channels are routed through.

others: Any other Pan Mode in the popup menu provides the *Pan Amount* slider plus a disclosure triangle for the Surround Panner.

Audio Enhancements

After you have set the Channel Configuration, panned it correctly and set the basic level, you might want to do some minor tweaking to your audio Clip without loading effects modules yet. FCPx provides the default Module "Audio Enhancements" just for that purpose. It includes 4 modules:

- ▶ **Graphic Equalizer:** Set an EQ to tweak the frequency response.
- ▶ **Loudness:** Adjust the overall Loudness (this is basically a Compressor function).
- ▶ **Background Noise Removal:** Remove some background noise (this is basically an Expander/Gate function).
- ▶ **Hum Removal:** Remove 50Hz or 60Hz hum noise caused by ground loops (this is similar to a notch filter).

The *Audio Enhancements* Module has three sections:

❶ **Header**: with the Show/Hide button, Reset button and Keyframe menu button.

❷ **Equalization**: with the Preset popup menu plus the EQ button that opens the Equalizer in a separate floating window.

❸ **Audio Analysis:** Displays the status of the Audio Analysis (see below) and a button (right arrow) that changes the Inspector window to the *Audio Enhancements* window which displays the remaining three modules. The Audio Enhancements window has a left arrow button in the upper left corner that switches the window back to the Inspector.

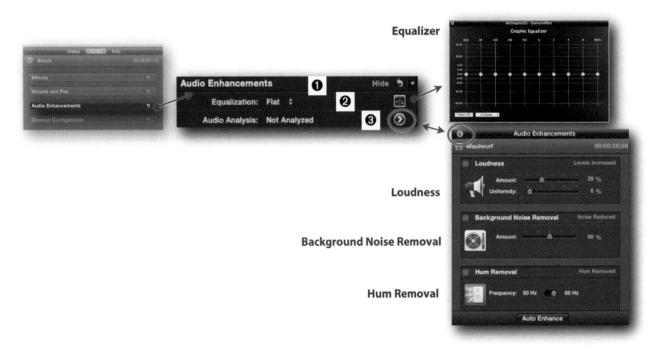

You can toggle the Audio Enhancements window for the selected audio Clip directly with the following commands:

 From the Enhancements popup menu (magic wand) toggle the command *Show/Hide Audio Enhancements*.

 Use the Key Command *cmd+8*

Enhancements popup menu

➡ Equalizer

The Equalizer section only has two items, the Equalization popup menu and the button to open the EQ window. The popup menu lists several items:

❶ **Flat**: This means the EQ is bypassed.

❷ **"EQ Presets"**: There are 8 Presets for specific situations that you can try. If you have the EQ window open then you can see what the adjustments are.

❸ **Custom**: This item is selected if you made your own adjustments in the EQ window.

❹ **Match**: This is a special feature if you want to match the sound characteristics (EQ) of a specific audio Clip that you like to another Clip.

The EQ window can be switched between a 10 band EQ (default) and a 31 band EQ ❺. Drag the individual slider up or down to set the level of a band ❻ or enter the level numerically in the entry box in the lower right corner ❼ for the selected frequency band.

The *"Flatten EQ"* button ❽ resets all the sliders to 0dB.

You can leave multiple EQ windows open to make adjustments to two or more audio Clips while playing. The window header displays the name of the Clip it belongs to ❾. An exception to the single window GUI concept.

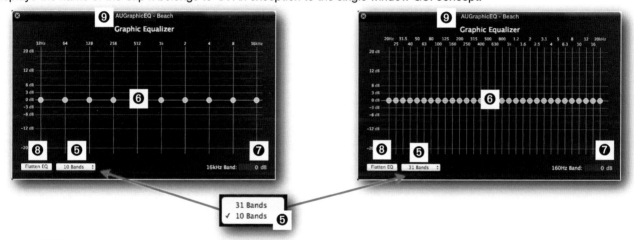

Match EQ

Sometimes you want one audio clip to sound like some other audio clip. For example, you have a poor sounding music cue that you want to sound like a great sounding music cue. Or you have two video clips that where shot on different days and they sound differently because the microphone was not correctly placed or it was a different microphone altogether. In those cases you have two options. You have a lot of experience and know what frequency bands to tweak or you do a trial and error. FCPx provides a third option: Match EQ.

These are the easy steps (the procedure is based on computer analysis, so your milage may vary):

☑ Select the target Clip that you want to adjust.

☑ You can initiate Match Audio in different ways:

Enhancements Menu

- Select Match from the EQ Preset menu
- Select *Match Audio* from the Enhancements Menu button
- Select from the Main Menu *Modify ➤ Match Audio...*
- Use the Key Command *sh+cmd+M*

- The Viewer changes to a split screen and displays a message with a Cancel button:
  "Choose a clip that has the audio you want to match"

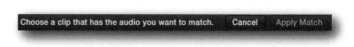

☑ Move the mouse over the source audio Clip that you want to use as the model.

• The mouse cursor adds a little EQ icon and the Skimming bar.

☑ Click the source audio.

• The text under the Viewer now displays the blue "*Apply Match*" button.

Choose a clip that has the audio you want to match. Cancel **Apply Match**

☑ Click the *Apply Match* button.

• The matched EQ has been applied to the target audio Clip.

• The Module header changes to display the active" *Choose*" button. Click it if you want to repeat the process from step 3.

• The Module header now displays the EQ button again. This time however it opens the "Match EQ" plugin instead of the Graphics EQ. You can tweak those parameters further if you want.

➡ *Audio Enhancements*

Before getting into the details of the other three sections of the Audio Enhancements Module, let's recap a feature called "*Analyze and fix audio problems*". This is a checkbox that is part of the import procedure either in the Import File window or in the Preference window for drag-and-drop imports. The process can also be initiated later by choosing the "*Analyze and Fix..*" command from the Event Clip's Shortcut Menu.

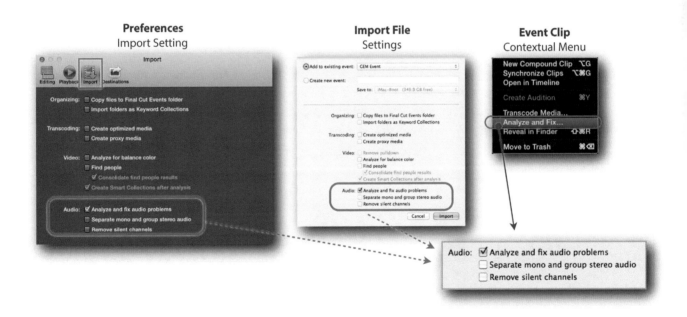

So what "Problems" is FCPx looking for? It looks for 3 specific problems, represented by the three remaining sections of the Audio Enhancements module:

▶ **Loudness:** Is the overall audio level in a good range or maybe there are too many peaks or the levels are too low?

▶ **Background Noise Removal:** Is there some constant background noise going on behind dialog?

▶ **Hum Removal:** Is there some noticeable 50Hz or 60Hz cycle hum present in the audio signal?

Here is the Audio Analysis procedure:

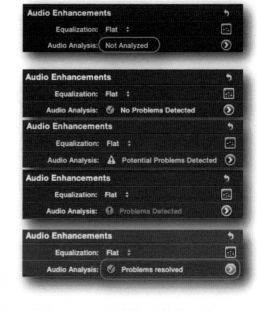

☑ If a selected Clips hasn't been analyzed, then the Audio Analysis section displays "*Not Analyzed*".

☑ If the selected Clips have been analyzed then the Audio Analyze section shows three possible results:

- **Green**: None of the three sections have any problem.
- **Yellow**: At least one of the section has potential problems.
- **Red**: At least one of the sections definitely has problems.

☑ If there was a (yellow or red) problem and that Module has been activated with the proper settings then the section displays a green check mark with the text "*Problems resolved*". The right arrow button is now blue to indicate that at least one of the Modules is turned on.

☑ Click the right arrow button to switch to the "Audio Enhancements" window. This toggles the Inspector window. To go back, click the left arrow in the upper left corner.

- If there were no problems, all the Modules have a green checkmark and the individual Modules are off. You still can turn them on manually and use them to try to improve the audio quality.

- If problems were detected, then that individual Module has a yellow or red mark and the Module is turned on with the settings that FCPx thinks will fix or reduce the problem. You can further adjust those settings or turn the Module off.

- Clicking the "*Auto Enhance*" button at the bottom of the Auto Enhancements window will turn yellow and red marked Modules on. You can also select that command from the Enhancements Menu *Auto Enhance Audio.*

Each Module indicates its status with the color icon.

no problems	potential problems	definite problems	"problem solved"

Please note that any changes made in those Modules will be reflected instantly in the audio waveform of the Timeline Clip.

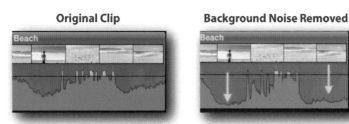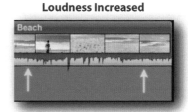

Original Clip **Background Noise Removed** **Loudness Increased**

Media Browser

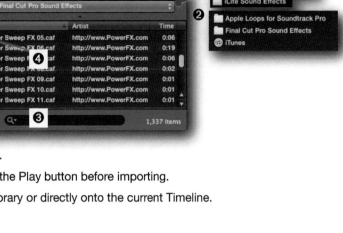

Media Browser

You can import Media Files (audio only or video files containing audio) through the standard import procedure or by dragging those files directly from the Finder to the FCPx window.

There is however one specific import procedure that is for audio clips only: Dragging files from the Media Browser, the "Music and Sound" Browser to be specific. The procedure is straight forward:

❶ Select the "Music and Sound" tab from the Toolbar. That will open the Media Browser window.

❷ The popup menu displays the current iTunes library plus any installed sound library that FCPx recognizes.

❸ You can search the available files and preview them with the Play button before importing.

❹ Drag the selected file(s) either to an Event in the Event Library or directly onto the current Timeline.

Record Audio

Another way to get audio into your Project is to record directly into FCPx. This comes in very handy when you want to record some quick voiceover audio into your project during editing. The procedure is very simple:

Open the Record Audio window from the Main Menu *Window* ➤ *Record Audio* (You can also assign a Key Command for that).

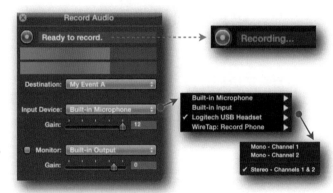

Make the selection and record:

Record button. Click on it or hit the *space* key to toggle Recording on/off (or hit the Play button in the Viewer).

The meters let you monitor the input level to avoid clipping.

Destination: The popup menu displays all the available Events. Choose the Event you want to assign the new audio file to.

Input Device: The popup menu displays all the available Input Sources connected to your computer. The menu provides a submenu to select a specific channel from that input device.

Gain: The slider lets you adjust the sensitivity for the input device.

Monitor: The popup menu displays all the available Output Destinations connected to your computer. The menu also provides a submenu to select a specific channel for that output device. Leave the checkbox unchecked to mute the output device and avoid possible audio feedback.

Gain: Set the monitor output level.

The following will happen when you hit record:

☑ Playback starts at the Playhead position.

☑ The audio from the selected Input Device will be recorded as an aiff into the selected Event's *Original Media* folder. The name of the file will start with "*VoiceOver-0*" and count up with each following recording.

☑ An Event Clip will be created in the selected Event for that audio file and named "*Voiceover 1*". Interesting that the Event Clip starts to count from 1 but the Source Media File starts from 0.

☑ That Event Clip will be placed on the Timeline Clip always as a Connected Clip starting at the Playhead position. If there was no Clip on the Primary Storyline, a Placeholder Clip will be created that the Voiceover clip connects to.

☑ The Clip will be assigned the Role "*Dialogue*".

SMPTE Reader

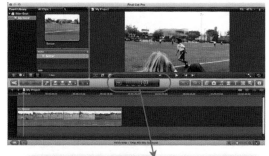

The Audio Meter Display has either 2 or 6 tracks depending on the Project property.

Click to toggle the Audio Meter window on-off. It extends to the right of the Timeline.

The Background Tasks Display indicates the percentage how much of the current background tasks has been completed.

Click to toggle the Background Tasks Window

The SMPTE Clock displays mainly the position of the Playhead or Skimmer and corresponds with the Viewer window. This could be either from the Event or the Project.

Besides that, it has multi-purpose functionality for displaying various time information and edit values.

➡ *Gray SMPTE*

- Displays the Playhead or Skimmer position.
- Displays the start position of a Connected Clip while dragging (not a Primary Storyline Clip).

➡ *Numeric Input Device*

The SMPTE Reader also functions as a numeric input device to enter a positive or negative time value. Use the *period* key as a separator h.m.f and the *esc* key to cancel the input.

There are two ways to input numbers. Either you *click* on the SMPTE Reader or you start pressing the + or - key:

◉ Click on the SMPTE

- *Click once* on the Display or press *ctr+P* for the Move Playhead command:
  It will reset the time display and show a blue Playhead instead of the Audio Meter on the right. Now type + or - and the time you want to move the Playhead to the left or right.

- *Click twice* on the Display to change the duration of a selected Clip. Keep in mind that this second click only works if a Clip is selected:
  The Display will show the duration of the Clip. Now type + or - and the amount of time you want to change the duration.

◉ Press + or - and a number

> **Nothing selected**: The entered value will move the Playhead.
>
> **Clip selected**: The entered value will move the selected Clip.
>
> **Edit Point selected**: The entered value will move the selected Edit Point.

What is Displayed/Controlled

Play Full Screen

Move Playhead
to the previous Edit Point
Play - Pause
Move Playhead
To the next Edit Point

The Transport Control buttons in the Viewer window affect either the selected Clip in the Event Browser or the Project Timeline whatever has key focus. The left upper corner of the Viewer indicates what is "feeding" the Viewer at the moment.

Viewer and Event Viewer

If the second Viewer, the Event Viewer, is displayed, then its controls will affect the selected Event Clip and the main Viewer's control will affect the Timeline regardless of the key focus.

The Navigation Controls can also be accessed from the Menu *View* ➤ *Playback* or with Key Commands.

The pre and post roll time for the "Play Around" command are set in the *Preferences* ➤ *Playback* window.

The standard "*J K L*" keys also work: *J* plays backwards *K* stops, *L* plays forward (press multiple times to increase speed).

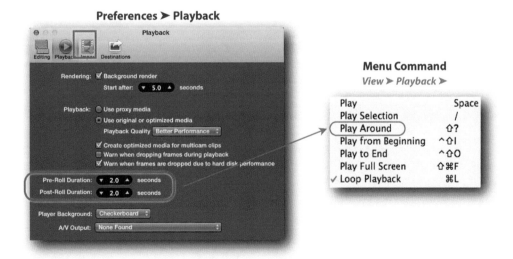

Preferences ➤ Playback

Menu Command
View ➤ *Playback* ➤

Play	Space
Play Selection	/
Play Around	⇧?
Play from Beginning	^⇧I
Play to End	^⇧O
Play Full Screen	⇧⌘F
✓ Loop Playback	⌘L

🔵 Full Screen

Please be aware that there are two "Full Screen" commands.

▶ **Enter Full Screen** (in the Window Menu): Switches the Viewer to Full Screen.

▶ **Play Full Screen** (in the *View* ➤ *Playback* Menu): Switches the Viewer to Full Screen and starts playback automatically.

Window Menu

✓ Final Cut Pro	
Enter Full Screen	^⌘F

View ➤ Playback Menu

 or

Play Full Screen	⇧⌘F

🎥 Zooming the Timeline

When zooming all the way in, the Playhead position displays a gray area in the SMPTE Timeline to indicate the range of 1 frame. The Skimmer will have that 1 frame "shadow" around it to indicate that 1 frame range.

Here are all the other Zoom commands that are also available from the View Menu

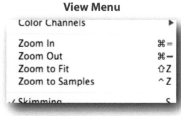

- ▶ **Zoom to Fit** everything: *Sh+Z*
- ▶ **Zoom In/Out**: *Cmd+Plus, cmd+Minus*. The Playhead or Skimmer (has priority) stays in "the picture" while zooming!
- ▶ **Zoom Tool**: *Click-drag* to select the zoom range or *click* in the Timeline to zoom step by step or *opt+click* to step out.
- ▶ **Zoom Slider**: Move the slider in the lower right corner of the Timeline window or click on the magnifier. Open the Clip Appearance window that includes a *Clip Height* slider.

Navigation

➡ *Playhead*

This is the bar that moves across the Timeline in the Project (red bar) or across the Event Clip in the Event Browser (white bar). It indicates the position where the playback starts when hitting the play button and moves along during playback. Please note that a "parked" Playhead in the Timeline is white when Skimming is activated.

- ▶ *Dragging* along the upper Time Ruler of the Timeline slides the Playhead. This will scrub the video but not the audio portion.
- ▶ *Clicking* on the upper Time Ruler of the Timeline forces the Playhead to jump to that position (can be used with any cursor tool)
- ▶ *Clicking* in the Timeline area (not on a Clip) will also place the Playhead there but might have different "side effects" with cursor tools other than the Select tool.
  - *Click* on a Clip will select the Clip (also deselecting any current Clip selection) but not move the Playhead.
  - *Opt+click* on a Clip will select the Clip and move the Playhead to that position.
- ▶ Pressing the Key + or - will change the SMPTE Reader to indicate that you can enter a numeric time value to move the Playhead by that amount or *click* on the SMPTE Reader before hitting the plus or minus key. Be sure that no Clip is selected because that would move the Clip and not the Playhead. Press *ctr+P* will also enable the input method.
- ▶ *Click* on an Event Clip will place the curser there and keep any current Range selection. *Opt+Click* on an Event Clip will place the Playhead there but deselects any Range selections.

➡ **Skimmer (Skimming or Clip Skimming)**

When activated (Key Command *S*), the red Skimming bar will be displayed at the cursor position and video and audio will be scrubbed along the Clip(s) when moving the mouse across. The audio portion can be deactivated independently in the View menu (Key Command *sh+S*).

- ▶ Moving the Skimmer will scrub the Project Timeline, the filmstrip in the Project Library or any Clip in the Event Browser.
- ▶ The Event Browser can display a Skimmer info window to display Keywords, Marker and time info (*View ➤ Show Skimmer Info*).
- ▶ *Clicking* while in Skimming mode will move the Playhead to that click position.
- ▶ Starting playback (Key Command *space*) when the Skimmer is visible will move the Playhead to that position and start playback.

➡ **Key Commands**

All the following commands are available from the *Mark* Menu.

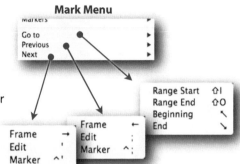

- ▶ Go to the **Beginning** of the Timeline: Key Command *home* or Menu Command *Mark ➤ Go To ➤ Beginning.*
- ▶ Go to the **End** of the Timeline: Key Command *end* or Menu Command *Mark ➤ Go To ➤ End.*
- ▶ Go to next **Clip Boundaries**: Key Command *arrow up* and *arrow down* or Key Command *;* and *'* (also available as buttons in the Viewer window).
- ▶ Go to next **Frame**: Key Command *arrow left* and *arrow right.*
- ▶ Go to next 10 **Frame**: Key Command *sh+arrow left* and *sh+arrow right.*
- ▶ Go to next **Sub Frame:** Key Command *cmd+arrow left* and *cmd+arrow right.*
- ▶ Go to next **Marker**: Key Command *ctr+;* and *ctr+'*

Timeline Index

Another navigation tool is the Project's Timeline Index. Open it with its own button on the bottom Toolbar or use the Key Command *sh+cmd+2.*

This window shows a chronological list of all the Timeline Clips (Clips tab), all the Tags (Tags tab) that are used in the Timeline or the existing Roles (Roles tab). It provides Filter buttons at the bottom of the window to narrow down the listed items and a search box to look for specific Clips or Tags used in the Timeline.

- ▶ A white Playhead moves vertically that corresponds with the Playhead position on the Timeline.
- ▶ Selecting any item in the list will move the Playhead in the Timeline and select the Clip or its Range with a gray border.

I will also get into more details about the Timeline Index in the manual *"Final Cut Pro X - The Details".*

Basics

Once you are done editing your project, you have to do the final step and "export" it. This is the process of saving the project to a differently formatted file for a specific purpose.

- Play the file with a specific app other than FCPx. For example, QuickTime Player, iTunes, on the web, etc.
- Play the file on a specific device. For example iPad, Apple TV, etc.
- Use the file on a specific application to further work on it. For example Compressor, Web Design, etc.

Export vs Share

The Export process is common in most content-creation applications where you work on a project in a proprietary format (video, song, graphics, etc) and at the end export it to a file format that can be opened (read, played) by other applications. Although this step is similar in various applications, the terminology varies. These are the most often used commands.

- Save as...
- Export...
- Share...
- Bounce...

It seems that Apple has tried to establish the term Share in all of their apps, and even has a system wide Share Button now found on their desktop applications (OSX) and also on their iDevices (iOS). Many Mac apps even have a dedicated Share Menu that lists all the different "export" options. Early FCPx versions also had this Share Menu but since version 10.0.6 the commands have moved back to the File Menu with a much improved interface. After all, this is a file management procedure.

Three Export Procedures

FCPx provides three different export procedures. They are all listed under the File Menu.

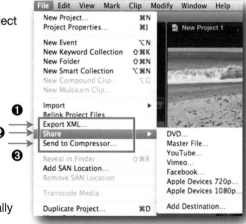

File Menu

❶ Export XML

This procedure is actually called an "Export". It creates an XML file of your Project or Event that can be used by applications for specific tasks.

❷ Share

This is the main export procedure that creates a media file of your Project (or Event Clip) in a wide variety of formats.

This command has a dynamic submenu that lists all the (pre-configured) Destinations.

❸ Send to Compressor

This is an "internal handshake". The current Project will be handed over internally on your computer to Apple's Compressor app (if installed) and opens there automatically, ready to be used in that app. Compressor 4 provides more detailed settings and formatting options to create specific media files.

To learn more about this cool "swiss army knife" app, check out my book "Compressor 4 - How it Works"

Now let's concentrate on the main procedure, *Share*.

Concept

The concept of exporting a Project or even an Event Clip in FCPx is very elegant and simple but yet extremely powerful. It uses *Destinations*.

> **Destinations = Export Presets**

- FCPx provides 12 Destination Types ❶ plus a special Destination Type, the "Bundle" ❷.

- These Destination Types are available in the Preferences window under the Destinations tab ❸ by selecting the "Add Destination" item in the Sidebar on the left ❽.

- Each of the 12 Destination Types, representing a specific kind of export procedure, provides a set of parameters for that procedure. The default values for those parameters can be modified later.

- The Sidebar ❹ on the left represents the list of the actual Destinations (Presets that contain the export instructions) which are used to export your Project (or Event Clip). A default selection of Destinations is already listed there.

- You can add new Destinations to the Sidebar by *dragging* any Destination Type onto the Sidebar ❾ or by *double-clicking* on a Destination Type. You can move the items in the Sidebar around to arrange them in the preferred order and also rename them. Please note that you can drag a specific Destination Type multiple times to the Sidebar. They then become individual Destinations of the same type that you can configure differently.

- The content of the Sidebar is displayed (mirrored) in two locations in FCPx representing the actual Share commands: The Share Menu ❺ in the File Menu and the Share Button Menu ❻ when pressing the Share Button on the Toolbar. Later, you initiate an export by selecting any of those Destinations in that menu.

- The Plus ❼ button at the bottom of the Sidebar selects the "*Add Destination*" item ❽ which displays all the 12 Destination Types plus the Bundle Destination ❷ so you can add new Destinations to the Sidebar.

- Delete any Destination from the Sidebar by selecting it and press the minus button ❼ or simply hit the *delete* key.

- Configure any Destination in the Sidebar by selecting it. Its parameters are then displayed in the right pane.

Configure a Destination

The configuration of a Destination is set on three levels.

- **Level 1**: Each of the 12 original Destination Types has a default configuration for their available parameters.

- **Level 2**: Once you drag a Destination Type onto the Sidebar, you make it available as a unique Destination, displayed in the Share Menu. Selecting any of those Destinations in the Sidebar ❷ displays its parameters on the right pane ❸. In that configuration window, you can change the default values of that Destination to fit your own needs.

- **Level 3**: Later when you actually use a specific Destination from the Share Menu for exporting a Project, you have again the opportunity to adjust the parameter values before starting the export.

Configuring the Destinations is very simple:

❶ Go to the *Preferences ➤ Destinations* window. You can also select "*Add Destination...*" from any of the two Share Menus, which opens the Preferences window.

❷ In the Sidebar, select the Destination that you want to configure.

❸ The right pane now displays all the available parameters and their current values for that Destination.

▶ Make the necessary changes. No Save command is required.

Configure a Bundle

A Bundle is a special Destination, like a macro. It is displayed as a folder that can include multiple Destinations. The concept is pretty simple. When you export a Project to a Bundle, that Project will be exported to all the Destinations in that Bundle at once. For example, you can publish a Project to multiple social media sites (even different accounts on the same social media site) or export a Project with different resolutions (low, medium, high).

The setup could not be simpler:

❶ Go to the *Preferences ➤ Destinations* window or select "*Add Destination...*" from any of the two Share Menus.

❹ Select "Add Destination" from the Sidebar.

❺ *Drag* the default Bundle Type to the sidebar. The Bundle in the Sidebar is actually a folder with a disclosure triangle.

❻ *Drag* any Destination Type onto that folder.

❼ You can even *drag* existing Destinations from the Sidebar onto that Bundle folder.

▶ The standard commands are available as expected: re-order by *dragging* Destination up and down, *opt+dragging* for duplicating. Select and delete or *click* and rename. Everything is straight forward and very logical.

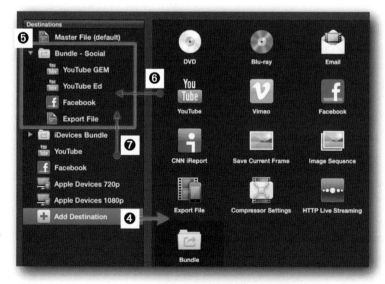

▶ Of course, you can configure each Destination in a Bundle by selecting it and configuring it the same way.

Configuration Window

Now let's look at each Destination Type's parameters that are displayed in the right pane.

➡ *Save Current Frame*

This is the easiest Destination. It lets you export the current frame at the parked Playhead position. Choose a specific graphics file format from the popup menu.

➡ *Export File*

This might be the most used export Destination. It exports the Project as a new Media File. The configuration pane has six parameters with popup menus to choose their value from. The displayed values vary depending on the setting of the first parameter, the *Format*. The value items on the Format popup menu are divided into two groups:

🌑 **Format**

  ▶ **Mastering:** Any of the three options can be used when exporting the Project as a master file, the final product of your video, or for further processing in another app. A Destination that has any of these three Format items selected will display a filmstrip icon in the Share Menu.

  ▶ **Publishing:** Any of those three options will also create a media file. They are optimized for playing the media file on specific devices (Apple Devices, Computer, Web Hosting). Destinations that have any of these Format items selected display a computer screen icon in the Share Menu.

🌑 **Video codec**, **Resolution** and **Audio file format** determine the actual format of the new media file.

🌑 **Include chapter marker** checkbox embeds any Chapter markers that are available in the Project. They can be used to better navigate the video file later.

🌑 **Open with** determines what happens to the output file after it is created. Besides "Do Nothing", the options are:

  ▶ Open with a specific app. For example, open the file with QuickTime Player once the export is completed.

  ▶ Add it automatically to a specific iTunes playlist of your iTunes Library. They are all listed in the popup menu.

  ▶ Publish it to the Media Browser in FCPx so you can re-import the new media file via drag-and-drop from inside FCPx.

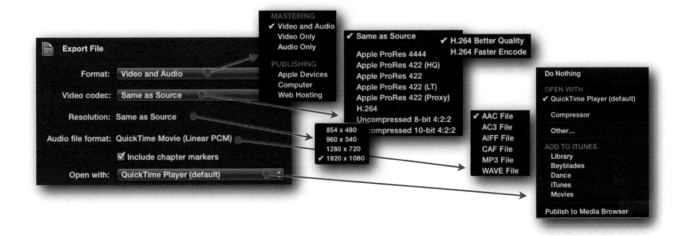

➡ **You Tube** 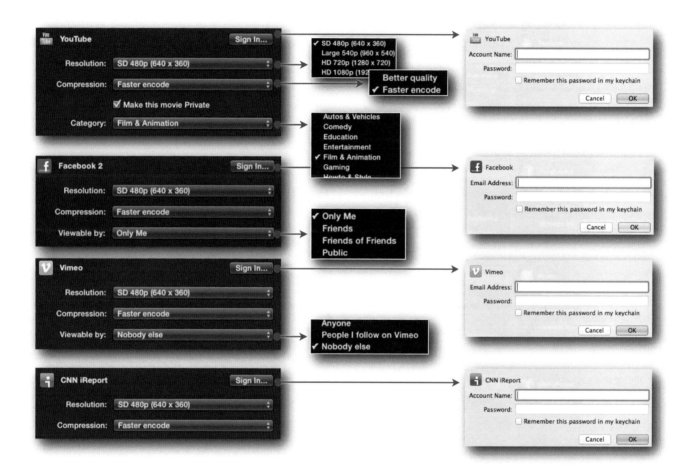 YouTube **Facebook** Facebook **Vimeo** Vimeo **CNN iReport** CNN iReport

These four Destination Types enable you to export your project and publish it directly to one of the social media sites. No extra step is needed to do the publishing after the export. The Destination settings also can include your login information. The settings page for the four social media sites are similar.

- When you drag the Destination Type to the Sidebar for the first time, a login window will popup. Here you can enter the name and password for the account you plan to upload the video to. With the checkbox "Remember this password in my keychain" you can store the login info so you don't have to enter it every time you export to that Destination.

- **Sign In**: This button opens the same login window, in case you want to change it later.

- **Resolution**: The available items on this popup menu are the same for all four Destinations.

- **Compressor**: Choose between *Better quality* and *Faster encode*. It is the same menu for all four.

- *Site Specific*: The last parameter values are specific for the individual social media site.

➡ **Email**  Email

The Email Destination is very convenient when you want to quickly attach your exported video file to an email. The configuration page provides only two parameters:

- Resolution: Select from the popup menu.

- Compression: Better quality versus Faster encoding.

Once the encoding is done, a new email will open in the Mail app with the exported media file attached and the Project name in the Subject line.

➡ DVD / Blue-ray

These two Destinations let you create a video DVD or video Blue-ray from your Project. It even provides basic authoring tools right in the Configuration pane with some animated templates. Please note that you can use the Chapter Markers as subtitles.

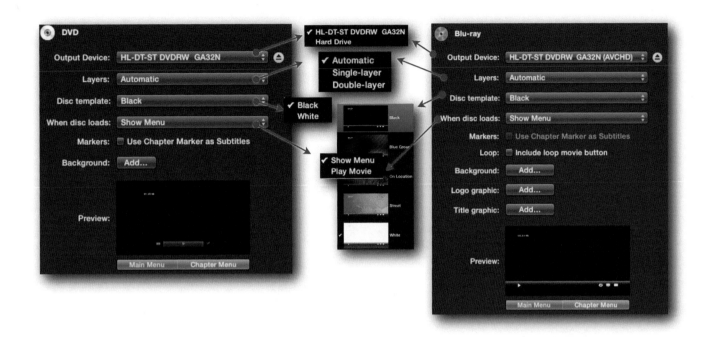

➡ Image Sequence

This Destination is used to create a series of images (individual frames) from your video project to be used in an animated video scene. The popup menu lets you choose the image format.

➡ HTTP Live Streaming

This Destination is used to create the media and html files required to make your video available on a website via HTTP Live Streaming.

The export can create up to three files, optimized for streaming over Cellular - WiFi or Broadband.

➡ *Compressor Settings*

I mentioned earlier that the File menu provides a separate Export command "Send to Compressor". This allows you to open the current project in Compressor and perform the actual export in the Compressor app which provides more detailed configuration options.

The "Compressor Settings" Destination on the other hand utilizes the power of Compressor without opening the app. Compressor has its own pre-configured export presets, called "*Settings*". FCPx lets you use those settings by assigning one of those specific Settings to a *Compressor Settings* Destination. And that is the only available parameter in the configuration page. It opens the Settings window where you can choose which Compressor Setting you want to assign to that Destination.

Of course if you don't have Compressor installed on your computer, you will get a friendly reminder.

➡ *Bundle*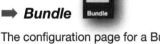

The configuration page for a Bundle is different because, as we have seen already, a Bundle is technically not a Destination but a collection of individual Destinations.

Therefore, the configuration page displays all the parameters of all the included Destination's configuration pages. This lets you make adjustments in one long list. You can also select a Destination inside a Bundle to display only that configuration page.

Attention

Please keep in mind that all the settings you configure for the various Destinations can be modified during the actual export when you use any of the Destinations. This makes sense, because you don't have to go back to the Preferences window for that. However, as we will see in the next section, any changes made for a Destination during the export will be saved to that Destination.

So be aware, the Destination you configure in the Preferences window can be overwritten in the Share Window.

Shortcut Menu

Ctr+click on any Destination in the Sidebar to open the Shortcut Menu with extra commands.

Destination: Shortcut Menu

- ▶ **Revert to Original Settings**: This changes the parameter values of the selected Destination(s) to the values of the original Destination Type.

- ▶ **Make Default**: The Destination that is marked the "Default" can be opened in FCPx with the Key Command *cmd+E* without the need to access the Share Menu.

- ▶ **Duplicate**: Duplicates the selected Destination(s).

- ▶ **Delete**: Deletes the selected Destination(s).

- ▶ **New Bundle From Selection**: Select any Destination (standard *cmd+click*) to move it into a new Bundle.

- ▶ **Restore Default Destinations**: This removes all your custom Destinations in the Sidebar and restores the initial list of Destinations that were there after a new FCPx install. You will be warned about those "consequences".

➡ *Default Destination*

You can make any Destination the default Destination, even a Bundle. The default Destination is marked with the word "*(default)*" at the end of its name.

This is the Destination that is used when starting the export procedure with the Key Command *cmd+E.*

Destinations: Import - Export

Destinations can easily be exchanged with other FCPx users or between different computers. It is so simple, it doesn't even require a separate command.

- ◉ **Export**: Just *drag* a Destination from the Sidebar to a Finder window or the Desktop. A FCPx Destination file will be created that includes all the settings. The file has the extension *.fcpxdest*. You can move that file to any location and import it to any FCPx application.

- ◉ **Import**: Just *drag* a FCPx Destination file from the Finder into the Sidebar of the Preferences window which will create a new Destination based on the file's configuration.

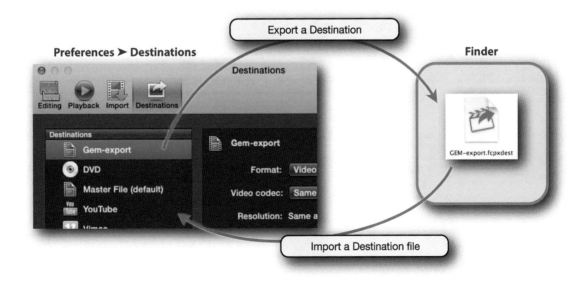

Share a Project

Now let's look at the actual export procedure when using any of those Destinations.

➡ *Export Steps*

☑ Choose **what** to export.

☑ Choose **how** to export by selecting a Destination from the Share Menu or use the Key Command *cmd+E.*

☑ Adjust the "**how** to export" in the Share Window.

☑ Start the export process.

What to Export

First, let's look at the source options, what to export.

💀 Entire Project

This lets you export the entire Project. You can start the export process from the current Timeline ❶ or by selecting a Project (its filmstrip) ❷ from the Project Library. Make sure that it is the Key Window (which means, it is selected).

💀 Section of the Project

You can select only a section of your current Project that you want to export. Just set a Range ❸ on the Primary Storyline with the Range tool or by defining an in and out point with the Key Commands *I* and *O* . The Project will now be exported only from the in point to the out point of the defined Range.

💀 Event Clip

You can also export any Event Clip ❹ from the Event Browser. Especially with Compound Clips, this is very useful.

💀 Section of an Event Clip

Also with an Event Clip, you can limit the export to a defined Range ❺ of the Event Clip.

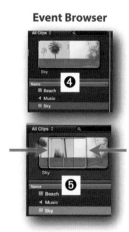
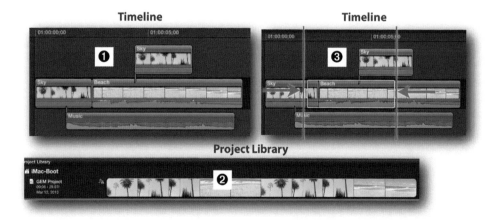

Roles

Besides the duration of the exported source (Project or Clip), you can also define specific Roles that you want to export. This is useful and very powerful for exporting Stems which I explain in the second book "Final Cut Pro X - The Details".

Share Window

Once you select the source (what you want to export) and have selected the Destination from the Share Menu, the next window will popup, the Share Window. This is where you make the final adjustments before starting the export process.

The window title displays the name of the Destination you chose for the export. Here are the other elements of this window.

❶ File Information

The strip at the bottom displays what format the exported file will have. The frame size and frame rate, audio channels and sample rate, duration, output file type, and the estimated file size. If you export a Range of your Project or Clip, then the icon next to the displayed duration is a Range icon ❽ instead of a clock icon.

Some Destinations will display the Compatibility Icon ❻: It opens a list with all the devices that can play the exported file.

❷ Video

Move the mouse over the image to skim the video that you are about to export. Video Skimming is always on but Audio Skimming has to be activated in the View Menu (Key Command *sh+S*).

❸ Info Tab

Under this Tab, you can view and modify the Share Attributes. These are metadata that will be embedded with the exported file. I will discuss this feature, the configuration and metatdata in the metadata chapter of book 2.

- ▶ Title: This will be the name of the exported file.
- ▶ Description
- ▶ Creator
- ▶ Tags

❹ Settings Tab

Under this Tab, you can view and modify the same parameters as in the configuration page we saw earlier when configuring the Destinations in the Preferences window. Please note that any changes made here will also change the Destination configuration in the Preferences window.
If the current Destination is a Bundle (with multiple Destinations), then the bottom of the Share Window displays two arrows that let you step through the individual Destinations ❼. The Settings tab will display the currently selected Destination.

❺ Share or Next button

The button that starts the final export process is labeled *Next* or *Share* depending on the current Destination. An additional window may prompt you to select a file location in the Finder.

You can think of the whole export process as three steps: before - during - after.

Before the export

You select **What** to export and by choosing the Destination you decide **HOW** to export.

During the export

Once the export starts, it is running in the background and you can continue to work on your project. Changing the project during the export won't affect the output file.

After the export

FCPx keeps a history of the exports and where the exported files are located.

During the Export

A major improvement to previous FCPx versions is that all the export tasks are now processed in the background and they are GPU accelerated. Once you start the export process, you can continue your work in FCPx and don't have to wait for the export to finish.

During the Export process, you can monitor its progress in two locations:

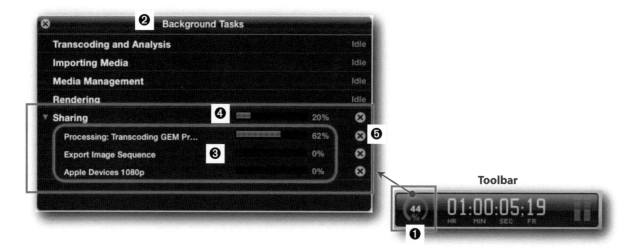

☻ The Percentage Meter

On the Toolbar left of the SMPTE display is a percentage meter ❶ which displays the background tasks activity. The number indicates what percentage of all the background tasks are completed. If you have only Sharing processes going on in the background, then this is the number that shows how much of those exports are done.

☻ Background Tasks window

Click on that percentage number in the Toolbar or use the Key Command *cmd+9* to toggle the Background Task window ❷. It displays all the individual background tasks with a progress bar if a process is going on.

If you have multiple exports processing at the same time, then each one is listed with their own progress bar and percentage number ❸ in addition to the total Share process ❹. This is also the place that lets you cancel a specific export process with the cancel button ❺ once it has been started in FCPx.

After the Export

Once the export is completed, you might think that FCPx is also done with it. However there are some useful features built in FCPx.

➡ *Share Icon*

Once a Project was exported, it will be tagged with a Share Icon, a little beam. This icon appears in the Timeline next to the Project Name ❶ and also in the Project Library next to the filmstrip ❷. *Click* on the icon in the Project Library to open the Share Inspector for that Project.

If the Project was modified after the last export, then a Share Icon changes to a beam with a warning sign ❹.

➡ *Share Inspector*

Any media file that FCPx creates during the export is stored to a default location (unless you choose a different location during the export). The location is inside a dedicated *Shared Items* folder ❺ that FCPx creates on your drive inside the Project folder (for exporting a Project) or inside the Event folder (for exporting an Event Clip).

That Shared Items folder also contains a little XML file, *ShareStatus.plist* ❻, that logs all the exports and the location of the exported file. That information is displayed (for Project exports only) in the Inspector ❼ under the Share tab. The exports are grouped by Destination type with a number, indicating how many exports have happened. Click on the number (or the Show button) to disclose the list ❽. Each export is listed as a separate list item with the date of the export and a magnifier icon to reveal the exported file in the Finder ❾.

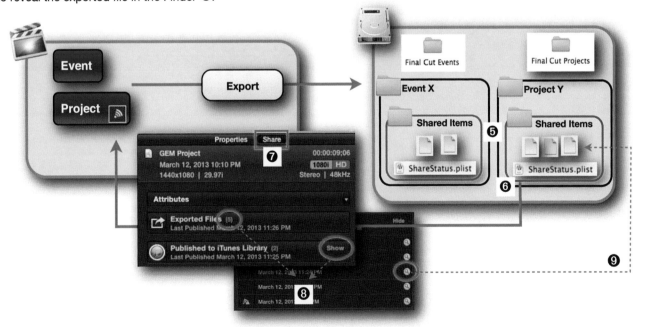

Command Set

The list of all the assigned Key Commands (keyboard shortcuts) in FCPx is called a *Command Set*.

- ▶ FCPx has one Default Command Set.
- ▶ You can modify that Default Command Set to create your own Custom Command Sets.
- ▶ This is done in the *Command Editor* window

Command Editor

The Command Editor is a floating window where you manage and modify Command Sets, the list of all assigned Keyboard Shortcuts used in FCPx. Open the window with any of the two commands:

 Main Menu *Final Cut Pro* ➤ *Commands* ➤ *Customize ...*

 Key Command *opt+cmd+K*

This will display a virtual keyboard and other controls. The window recognizes and displays exactly the type of keyboard that is connected to your computer.

Commands Menu

Let's have a look at the Main Menu *Final Cut Pro* ➤ *Commands* to understand the logic behind it:

- ▶ The Menu lists the default Command Set as *Default* under the "**Command Sets**" ❶ and any custom created command set under "**Custom Command Sets**" ❷.
- ▶ *Click* on any Command Set to make it active. The currently active Command Set has a checkbox ❸ next to it.
- ▶ *Click* on **Customize...** ❹ to open the Command Editor window. The Editor displays the currently active Command Set.
- ▶ The **Import...** and **Export...** ❺ In the menu lets you import and export Command Sets. They are stored as XML files with the file extension *.commandsets*. A Save Dialog lets you save the file to any location on your drive and they are not restricted by FCPx strict file location policies. This makes it easy to exchange Command Sets between users or different workstations.

The layout and functionality of the Command Editor is quite sophisticated:

➡ **Command List Pane**: This section lists the Key Commands. It has a sidebar on the left and a browser to the right.

❶ Command Groups: This area lets you restrict what is displayed in the browser next to it. You can display all Key Commands, only the ones assigned to commands in the various Main Menus, or display Key Commands grouped by functionality (Editing, Effects, etc). These groups have a color code that is also applied to the assigned keys on the virtual keyboard.

❷ Command Browser: This is the browser area that displays a list of all the Key Commands based on the selection in the Sidebar. The list has three columns (Command, Modifiers, Key). You can use their header to set a specific sort order. You can restrict the list even further by applying a search phrase in the search box ❸. The magnifying glass icon ❹ pops up a menu where you can select the field you are searching (Key Equivalent is the actual Keystroke, i.e. *sh+cmd+S*)

Click the Keyboard Highlight ❺ button  to highlight the keys on the virtual keyboard that are currently displayed in the Command Browser.

➡ **Detail Pane**: This area in the lower right switches between two different views depending what is selected.

❻ Command Detail: If you select any Command in the Command Browser, then this area will display a short description, explaining the function of that Key Command.

❼ Key Detail: If you select any key on the virtual Keyboard, then this area displays all the possible Modifier Key combinations ("Key Equivalent") for that key and the commands that are assigned to any combination.

➡ **Virtual Keyboard**: The dot on a Key tells you that it has an assignment. Select any combination of the Modifier Key buttons at the top ❽ to display the assignments with those modifier keys. The color indicates the Command Group (Effect, Editing, etc) it belongs to. A shaded key means that it is off limits due to a System Assignment. A yellow Helper Text displays a description of the assigned command when you move the mouse over a key.

💡 **Add Key Command**: Simply select a Command from the Command Browser and press the key combination on your real keyboard. You will get an alert window if that key assignment is already used.

💡 **Re-assign/Delete Key Command**: You can drag a Key on the Virtual Keyboard or the Token (the colored label representing the actual Command) on the Key Detail List to a new key on the Virtual Keyboard to re-assign that Key Command or drag it away from the window to delete that assignment (in a puff of smoke).

The popup menu ❾ in the left upper corner is similar to the Command Menu with the additional commands to Delete and Duplicate a Command Set. Please note that you can only name a Command Set when you duplicate it.

Conclusion

This concludes my "*Final Cut Pro X - How it Works*" manual. In the next manual "*Final Cut Pro X - The Details*", I will dive into more details of all the remaining topics and cover the more advanced features.

You can find more of my "Graphically Enhanced Manuals" on my website at: www.DingDingMusic.com/Manuals

Subscribe to my mailing list for updates and future releases: subscribe@DingDingMusic.com

All the titles are available as pdf downloads from my website, as printed books on Amazon.com and as Multi-Touch eBooks on Apple's iBookstore.

(languages: English, Deutsch, Español, 简体中文)

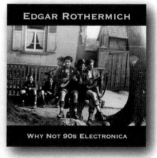

If you find my visual approach of explaining topics and concepts helpful, please recommend my books to others or maybe write a review on Amazon or the iBookstore. This will help me to continue this series.

Special thanks to my beautiful wife Li for her love and understanding during those long hours of working on the books. And not to forget my son Winston. Waiting for him during soccer practice always gives me extra time to work on a few chapters.

More information about my day job as a composer and links to my social network sites: www.DingDingMusic.com

Listen to my music on www.SoundCloud.com/edgar_rothermich/

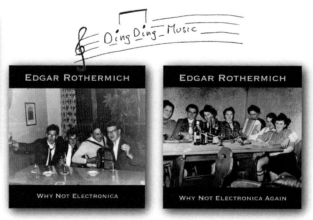

To contact me directly, email me at: GEM@DingDingMusic.com

Thanks for your interest and your support,

Edgar Rothermich

Made in the USA
Charleston, SC
18 September 2013